Praise for
Nothing Ventured, Everything Gained

"This is a true 'Street Fighters' book. For a long time, I have searched for a book that honestly documents the secret, proven techniques used by America's most successful entrepreneurs. Dr. Rao's book does this. Read it."

—Bill Winter, Co-Founder,
Merrill Custom Communications (Forbes
list of 100 Top Small Companies)

"Turn off your investor pitch deck and boot up your business from the bottom up. This book is a how-to guide for those who have experienced (or want to avoid) the perils and misguided frustrations of the VC world. Rao shatters the Silicon Valley myth that billion-dollar businesses are predicated on the venture-capital method and makes compelling and well-defended arguments that lend credence to delaying or avoiding VC capital altogether. Finally, the entrepreneur is empowered to build a business *and* reap the rewards."

—David M. Ochi, UCI Applied Innovation, Interim Director, New Ventures

"Dileep's new book, *Nothing Ventured, Everything Gained*, points out that entrepreneurs can build successful ventures with skills and smart strategies. It shows you how entrepreneurs like me did it without venture capital. If you want to build your business and stay in control, read this book. It is invaluable."

—Glen Taylor, Owner, Minnesota Timberwolves,
Minnesota Lynx, and *Star Tribune*, Founder, Taylor Corporation

"Dileep Rao's holistic approach to entrepreneurship is an impressive, comprehensive, and practical guide for budding entrepreneurs—whether they are striking out on their own or have come to the realization that successful managers must have an entrepreneurial mindset. The book explains why skills are needed before capital: Capital is limited, and entrepreneurial skills, not hopes, are what attract capital. This book describes the skills that more than 90 percent of entrepreneurs use to develop the right opportunity for growth and to design the right strategy for growth without venture capital. As a former entrepreneur, I thought that the focus on 'truths are myths' was especially relevant. I found the book to be pithy, practical, and to the point—a must-read for budding entrepreneurs."

—**Stephen T. Barnett, PhD, Professor of Marketing Emeritus, Stetson University**

"Instead of focusing solely on the opportunity, *Nothing Ventured, Everything Gained* lays out how the 99.98 percent of entrepreneurs who don't benefit from venture capital—and the balance who do—can build big businesses with skills and smart strategies before seeking VC. With proven examples, Dr. Rao shows how all entrepreneurs can build businesses, control them, and keep more of the wealth they create."

—**Ban Aase, Principal, Public Sector, CliftonLarsonAllen LLP**

"In his latest book, *Nothing Ventured, Everything Gained*, Dileep Rao illustrates how to build a unicorn company without venture capital. He proves VC money does not necessarily buy happiness or success, and shows how bootstrap innovation skills, missionary sales skills, frugal operations skills, and revolutionary visioning skills create the most successful companies."

—**Judy Corson, Co-Founder, Custom Research Inc.**

"Rao writes with insight and wisdom. He's a really smart guy providing really smart skills and strategies to grow a successful company without giving up control of one's venture."

—Dr. Raymond Smilor, Emeritus Professor of Entrepreneurship, Neeley School of Business, Texas Christian University

"With a quarter century of experience in financing the growth of hundreds of businesses, Dr. Rao has personally "walked the talk" in venture development. Now, using personal interviews and examples from some of America's most successful entrepreneurs, his book provides a growth map for entrepreneurs who don't get venture capital or could fail with it."

—William Rudelius, Professor Emeritus, Marketing, Carlson School of Management, University of Minnesota

"In Dileep Rao's insightful new book *Nothing Ventured, Everything Gained*, he demonstrates that while venture-backed startups (particularly those backed by substantial money from the major venture firms) get all the attention, the vast majority of startups do not use venture capital. Furthermore, he shows that even without a dime of venture capital, one can build a billion-dollar business. Along the way, Rao gives practical, experience-based advice on just how to do it.

—Mitch Maidique, Former President, Florida International University

How Entrepreneurs Create, Control, and
Retain Wealth Without Venture Capital

NOTHING
VENTURED,
EVERYTHING
GAINED

DILEEP RAO

AN INC.
ORIGINAL

Other Titles by Dileep Rao

*Handbook of Business Finance: Find Equity,
Debt, & Low-Cost Financing Intelligently*

*Finance Any Business Intelligently: How Entrepreneurs
can get the Right Financing from Smart Financiers*

*Business Plans Intelligently: Develop to Make Money.
Write to Raise Money*

*Bootstrap to Billions: Proven Rules from Entrepreneurs
who Built Great Companies from Scratch*

These titles are available online at the author's website:
www.dileeprao.com.

To my parents for the foundation.
To my wife and children for the inspiration.

An Inc. Original
New York, New York
www.inc.com

This work is being published under the An Inc. Original imprint
by an exclusive arrangement with Inc. Magazine. Inc. Magazine
and the Inc. logo are registered trademarks of Mansueto Ventures,
LLC. The An Inc. Original logo is a wholly owned trademark of
Mansueto Ventures, LLC.

Distributed by River Grove Books

Design and composition by Greenleaf Book Group
Cover design by Greenleaf Book Group
Cover image: ©maxsattana, 2018. Used under license
from Shutterstock.com

Cataloging-in-Publication data is available.

Print ISBN: 978-0-9991913-3-0

eBook ISBN: 978-0-9991913-4-7

First Edition

Contents

Introduction

Can smart entrepreneurs grow richer without smart money?

A popular myth is that growing ventures need venture capital (VC), which is also called smart money by the media. After 23 years as a financier (VC, debt, leases) and managing turnarounds, I was convinced of financiers' importance. But when I interviewed billion- and hundred-million-dollar entrepreneurs to learn their secret sauce, I was surprised.

Billion-dollar entrepreneurs, such as Bill Gates, Jeff Bezos, Mark Zuckerberg, Steve Ells, Michael Bloomberg, Bob Kierlin, Richard Schulze, and Kevin Plank, controlled their ventures by avoiding VC or delaying it until takeoff and proving their leadership skills. To do so, they got the right finance-smart skills and used the right finance-smart strategies.

In this book, I define a billion-dollar entrepreneur as the founder or cofounder of a startup who, while remaining involved in a leadership position, built the venture into over $1 billion in sales and valuation; and hundred-million-dollar entrepreneurs as those who built their firm from startup to over $100 million in sales and/or valuation.[*]

---

[*] Glen Taylor is the exception in this book. Mr. Taylor bought the company when it was very small and built it into a giant.

Venture capitalists are defined as institutional financiers (mainly limited partnerships or bank-owned small business investment companies) who invest a large amount of equity in the early stages of high-potential ventures. They normally seek control of the venture. (Unlike VCs, other early-stage investors, such as friends, family, angels, or alliance partners, either do not seek control or they invest smaller amounts.)

Entrepreneurs succeed by dominating their market. They create wealth by dominating big markets. They keep more of the wealth created by dominating big markets with *control*.

The Role of VC

Many believe that VC is essential to build a dominating, giant corporation, but venture capitalists (VCs) also want control. VCs seek control and often recruit professional executives (as CEOs) to replace entrepreneurs when the entrepreneurs have not proven their leadership skills. VCs did this with eBay. The proportion of entrepreneurs being replaced by VCs can be as low as 20 percent.[1] However, some have estimated the number in the top 50 VC-funded deals to be much higher.

By controlling or avoiding VC, billion-dollar entrepreneurs controlled the venture and the wealth created—and retained more of it. VC-delayers kept more of the wealth created than those who received VC early on. VC-avoiders kept the highest portion.

Billion-dollar entrepreneurial expertise helps the 99.9 percent of entrepreneurs who will not get VC and the approximately 0.08 percent who fail with VC to grow without VC. This expertise can also help the remaining 0.02 percent of entrepreneurs who profit from VC to delay getting it until after takeoff to control the venture and the wealth created.

This book discusses the business skills and strategies of America's finance-smart, billion-dollar entrepreneurs who started and built big businesses to dominate big markets.**

To grow with control, over 90 percent of them avoided or delayed VC (76 percent avoided, 18 percent delayed).

To grow without VC or with delayed VC, finance-smart entrepreneurs linked business and finance by developing finance-smart skills and using finance-smart strategies. By using the right skills and strategies, they evaluated the implications of every aspect of their business and adjusted the business for greater capital efficiency. With greater capital efficiency, finance-smart entrepreneurs stayed in control, created more wealth per dollar used, and kept more of the wealth created.

Finance-smart expertise helps entrepreneurs for two reasons:

- VC works for few, primarily only in Silicon Valley when industries are emerging.

- Finance-smart works for all, at all times, and everywhere.

Track Record: VC Works for Few

Historical data shows that VC is not essential to build giant companies. The capital-dependent VC strategy is justified for very few entrepreneurs and mainly in Silicon Valley.

VC works after evidence of potential, that is, after "Aha." Ninety-six to 98 percent of VC is invested after Aha.*** *Aha is that magic moment when the world sees potential—in the opportunity, strategy, or leadership. At Aha, customers see value, and financiers see returns!* This means

---

** The examples are from the VC age. The companies were started after the first VC fund was launched in 1946.

*** See pwcmoneytree.com for more information about VC funding practices.

that entrepreneurs need to know how to grow from startup until Aha without VC.

It is not easy to get VC; 99.95 percent of start-ups and 99.9 percent of all emerging businesses do not get VC. Only about 300 to 400 start-ups (from a pool of about 600,000 annually) and 3,000 to 4,000 ventures at all stages get VC financing each year. Most entrepreneurs will never get VC. They need to succeed without VC.

Few ventures succeed with VC. Only about 15 to 60 ventures become home runs each year. Nearly all the home runs are in Silicon Valley and were started when high-potential industries were emerging. These are companies like Google and Facebook, where many who are remotely connected with the venture become millionaires and those at the center of the flame become billionaires. Based on the assertion that about 20 percent of VC deals are successes, an additional 540 to 785 ventures succeed each year. In these successes, which do not become home runs, VCs get preference for their money and their returns, and the others share what's left over. The net result is that about 99.997 percent of entrepreneurs may not get VC or benefit from VC.

Very few VCs build home runs. Entrepreneurs assume that all VCs are successful since they have money to invest. In reality, about 4 percent of VCs earn high returns, since few VCs finance home runs. These top VCs earn 66 percent of the IPO (Initial Public Offering) profits of the VC industry. But even these few successful VCs fail on most of their deals. While some VCs do add value some of the time, many do not have much of a record of doing so. Instead of adding value, VCs (and the board of directors) may fire you and get someone else to run your venture, which can further dilute your interest in your company. This is what happened to Steve Jobs when he was fired from Apple. When this happens, you may not benefit even when your venture does well. Jobs was "luckier." In exile, he built Pixar and then returned to make Apple a great company.[2]

Venture capital firms have only succeeded in some areas. Practically all of the top 50 VCs have been in Silicon Valley because most of the billion-dollar entrepreneurs in Silicon Valley used VC but mainly after Aha! Billion-dollar entrepreneurs outside Silicon Valley seldom used VC.

Mark Zuckerberg was lured to Silicon Valley from Boston by an angel, but only after he was getting millions of users for Facebook. Venture capitalists came later.[3]

Venture capital has succeeded mainly when high-potential industries are emerging. Historically, VCs earned high returns from emerging, high-potential industries such as semiconductors, personal computers, biotechnology, and telecommunications in the 1970s and 1980s; Internet 1.0 in the 1990s; and Internet 2.0 in the 2000s. When there are no major industries at the emerging stage, VC returns have fallen.

Finance-Smart Works for All and Everywhere

Since funding is limited before Aha and VC works mainly in Silicon Valley for very few when high-potential industries are emerging, entrepreneurs need to be finance-smart to grow. This is what more than 90 percent of America's billion-dollar entrepreneurs did to avoid VC outside Silicon Valley and delay VC in Silicon Valley.

Being capital-intensive may be a risky strategy, since VC may not be available when you need it, or on the right terms, and it is difficult to switch from capital-intensity to capital-efficiency.

Entrepreneurs who get VC early lose control of their venture and the wealth created. Both are diluted by the VCs and the executives recruited into the venture. Billion-dollar entrepreneurs who got VC early and lost control kept only 7 percent of the wealth created. Those who delayed getting VC kept 16 percent. VC-avoiders kept 52 percent. To create wealth, control it, and retain more of it, all entrepreneurs can benefit by knowing how to grow without capital or with control of capital.

. . .

This book is divided into three sections.

Part 1 discusses the finance-smart skills that billion-dollar entrepreneurs had or developed to take off without VC.

Part 2 discusses the innovation strategies of finance-smart entrepreneurs for more potential per dollar. By finding the right opportunity, ventures can develop a sustainable advantage. But finding the right opportunity for high growth without capital is not easy.

Part 3 discusses business strategies used by finance-smart entrepreneurs for more edge per dollar. A business strategy includes the right combination of product, customers, and competitive advantage to help you grow, preferably with capital efficiency. The business strategy is often more important than the product, especially if the product can be imitated.

VCs mainly invest after the product and strategy have been proven and the business has momentum. Entrepreneurs need to start from a blank slate.

PART I

SKILLS TO SUCCEED WITHOUT VENTURE CAPITAL

> While entrepreneurs often think they can write a business plan, get VC, and become fabulously wealthy, this scenario is as likely as winning the lottery. Entrepreneurs can do better with the right skills to bring their venture to Aha when their potential is evident and VC is easier to get. But with the right skills, entrepreneurs may realize that they can grow without VC.

What skills do you need to start and build a high-growth venture?

One option is to get an idea, develop the product or service, and seek funding from angels to launch the venture. When the enterprise shows signs of potential, seek VC. The VCs hire a professional CEO whose job is to turn the venture into a Fortune 500 company or a home-run venture that is sold to a Fortune 500 company for billions. The entrepreneur recoups hundreds of millions or billions. This scenario is as rare as winning the lottery.

The reality is that 99.9 percent of ventures are unlikely to get VC. Eighty percent of those who get VC fail or barely break even. This means that nearly all entrepreneurs can benefit from knowing how to use the alternate option. This other option is to do it the way many billion-dollar entrepreneurs did in both Silicon Valley and outside.

Silicon Valley entrepreneurs had or obtained the skills to develop the opportunity, launch it with minimal resources from angels, and prove its potential. They got VC after their potential was evident to VCs, that is, after Aha.

Outside Silicon Valley, most entrepreneurs acquired takeoff skills to develop their product and launch their business. They used their skills and expertise to dominate their first market and then continued to grow to lead the national market. They mainly did it with skills and with Alt-VC, which includes debt, government financing, alliance funding, and any type of funding except VC because they did not want to lose control of their venture.

Entrepreneurs with the takeoff skills to build a business will do better than those who only have the skills to write a business plan and seek funding. By obtaining the skills to take off without VC, entrepreneurs have the choice to decide at a later stage whether or not they need VC to succeed and to get it with the right terms.

The reality is that all entrepreneurs can benefit by getting the skills to take off without capital because few get VC, fewer succeed with VC, and even fewer become wealthy with VC. More billion-dollar entrepreneurs have succeeded due to the right skills, rather than VC. The right skills are the following:

- Bootstrap innovation skills
- Missionary sales skills
- Frugal operations skills
- Revolutionary visioning skills

CHAPTER 1

Bootstrapping Innovation

What you sell is one of the most important decisions, along with how you sell and to whom. To develop the right product, the track record of billion-dollar entrepreneurs suggests that it helps to have skills to better satisfy customers' unmet needs in emerging trends, emerging markets, or emerging technologies.

"And we have always been shameless about stealing great ideas."
—Steve Jobs in a TV documentary, *Triumph of the Nerds* (1996)

Finding the right opportunity is the first step in developing your venture. To take off without capital, entrepreneurs need to have the skills to bootstrap their innovation.

Sam Walton knew how to operate stores in small towns. When the big-store format emerged, he had the skills and experience to operate a big store in small towns.

Steve Ells was a trained chef and wanted to open his own high-end restaurant. To earn some money, he started Chipotle to offer organic foods in a quick-serve setting.

Mark Zuckerberg and Bill Gates were programming mavens.

Most billion-dollar entrepreneurs developed their initial product or service using their skills—and did not need capital. Very little institutional venture capital is provided at the seed stage. In 2016, this amount was about $2 billion (according to pwcmoneytree.com), which is about 4 percent of the total U.S. VC funding. Only 1,428 deals were made, which is about 0.2 percent of U.S. startups. This suggests that most entrepreneurs will need to develop their opportunity without VC. They need to bootstrap or use limited funds available from friends, family, and angels. Even if angel funding is obtained, there is no assurance of getting institutional VC, so bootstrap innovation is advised.

Following are some billion-dollar entrepreneurial skills to bootstrap the opportunity for more advantage with less.

Identify and Satisfy Unmet Needs

Recognizing and satisfying unmet needs to *offer higher value* has been the hallmark of entrepreneurs. By understanding your market's unmet needs, you can sell customers the right products and services. Ever since the first entrepreneur appeared, the second entrepreneur asked, "How can I do it better or cheaper?" Better or cheaper is an unmet need. Customers want to save money or have more needs satisfied. But the key difference among high-performance entrepreneurs was that they had the skills to develop a solution with a long-term advantage. This helped to increase sales and margins, which is especially useful in the emerging stages of a company and industry. And customers are likely to buy faster with shorter sales cycles and at higher prices.

Kevin Plank built Under Armour by developing garments to make football players and all athletes more competitive. He focused on college football teams since he was familiar with many of them, having been a college football player himself. He focused on showing these players how his garments improved performance, which was important to them if they were to be drafted by the NFL.[1]

Glen Taylor (Taylor Corporation) started to catch brides' attention by developing a catalog of wedding invitations that was of similar quality to those from the leading companies. But Taylor found that brides wanted to reflect their personalities on their special day. Previously, the company's (and industry's) response had been to tell them "You can get what we have." Taylor, however, noticed that brides were not asking about price when wanting to satisfy their unique wishes. He decided to try to satisfy these customers by selling customized products at a higher price.

He was the first to offer cards based on the hot songs, movies, and other themes of the day. He offered additional colors that were in sync with the market and the industry. He helped brides coordinate all the colors in their wedding, including the paper products, invitations, bridal dresses, and more. Brides loved the idea and paid more for it. He could not keep up with demand. By satisfying the unmet needs of his customers, Taylor increased the size of his typical order by 5 percent and his profits by over 60 percent. His company took off. (For more about Taylor, see the last chapter.)

Emerging Technologies

Some entrepreneurs use their unique skills to develop their product or service to launch their business in emerging technologies. Established companies usually are not dominant in these emerging technologies, and the new ventures can gain a strong foothold before the dominant companies are aware of the opportunity—and the threat.

After World War II, as an electrical engineering student at the University of Minnesota's Institute of Technology, Earl Bakken (founder of Medtronic) would stop by the university's medical school and hospital to visit friends. He would repair their equipment on-site and realized that there was a business opportunity. So he and his brother-in-law started Medtronic to repair medical equipment on-site.

Medtronic's early days were agonizing and arduous. The venture's highest annual net income in the first decade was $10,400. To grow, Medtronic worked with physicians to develop custom-designed equipment for specific treatments. One of these physicians, Dr. C. Walton Lillehei, was using medical devices for the heart, but the devices would fail during power interruptions and thus adversely affect patients' lives. So Lillehei asked Bakken to develop a device that would work through power failures. Bakken experimented with various options and, in four weeks, came up with a solution based on a circuit in *Popular Electronics* for an electronic metronome. This pacemaker was attached to a child's heart the next day, heralding the dawn of the modern-day electronic medical device industry.

Emerging Industries

Emerging industries are usually based on changing markets, technologies, or demographics. They create new opportunities for entrepreneurs and offer an advantage to those who are willing to jump into a new industry.

Bob Noyce and Gordon Moore founded Intel at the dawn of the semiconductor age. Noyce was a co-inventor of the integrated circuit.

Bill Gates and Paul Allen knew how to write computer code for personal computers, which was a key skill in the emerging PC industry. The two had been working on PCs throughout high school.

Steve Jobs knew how to develop and market PCs and formed a partnership with Steve Wozniak, who had the technology skills. Wozniak developed the first few products sold by Apple.

Herbert Boyer and VC Robert Swanson founded Genentech at the dawn of the biotechnology trend. Boyer was a pioneer in recombinant DNA technology.

These successful entrepreneurs had functional skills in emerging industries, enabling them to become pioneers in their fields. Table 1 shows some major industries that have emerged in the last 50 years. This suggests that a key factor for highly successful entrepreneurs is to acquire technology skills in emerging industries or technologies— on their own or with partners.

TABLE 1. HOME RUNS BY TIMING AND EMERGING INDUSTRY

TIME	INDUSTRY	HOME RUNS (YEAR FOUNDED)
'60s	Semiconductors	Intel (1968), AMD (1969)
'70s	PCs	Apple (1976), Microsoft (1975)
'70s, '80s	Biotech	Genentech (1976), Amgen (1980)
'80s, '90s	Telecom/Optics	Cisco (1984), Ciena (1992)
'90s	Internet	eBay (1994), Google (1998)
'00s	Internet 2.0	Facebook (2004), Twitter (2006)

Improving an Emerging Industry

Many billion-dollar entrepreneurs got their start in emerging industries because they had skills in the industry. But they were not the first movers. When the industry emerged, they examined the leading products and improved upon them. They compared the benefits offered by the existing products with the unmet needs of the emerging market. This gave them a foothold, which they used to dominate the market. This suggests that first movers don't always win. Imitators and improvers can do better if the first movers haven't guessed right. In fact, first movers dominate only about 11 percent of the time.[2]

Larry Page and Sergey Brin used their expertise in programming to cofound Google when the Internet was just emerging.

Mark Zuckerberg was a programming expert when the online

linking industry emerged. He wrote the code for a linking site and improved on the existing business model by focusing on college students who wanted to meet others at their university, and Facebook took flight.

Taking Advantage of Emerging Trends

Emerging trends offer a boost for entrepreneurs. Emerging trends offer the prospect of entering when an industry is still forming. An emerging trend can be especially beneficial if large corporations find it difficult to jump on the trend without major disruptions to their existing business.

Richard Burke founded UnitedHealthcare (UNH) in the 1970s, when legislation was passed to promote health maintenance organizations (HMOs). There were already a few HMOs around the country, such as Kaiser and Group Health, which offered access to a limited number of staff physicians and had limited market appeal. The new concept involved building off private-practice doctors to provide medical care in new managed-care entities. Two key features of the new federal law—the HMO Act of 1973—were that it overrode the state laws that had historically inhibited organizations of this type from operating, and it required employers with 25 or more employees to offer at least one managed-care option. By capitalizing on this law and forming alliances with local medical associations, Burke developed UNH into the dominating company in medicine.

Amazon.com is a classic example of a young company that recognized an emerging trend. It has taken full advantage of the limits of store-based retailing in a web-based world. By understanding the emerging trend of online retail and using the strengths of the Internet, Jeff Bezos has been able to build one of the world's great disrupters, by focusing on excelling at the infrastructure of the Internet, along with selling products and services.[3]

• • •

Many entrepreneurs are under the impression that they can obtain a unique advantage from their opportunity—but few do. Most products or services can be duplicated by others.

To find an advantage, entrepreneurs need to know how to develop products that better satisfy unmet needs, especially in emerging industries, emerging trends, or emerging markets.

CHAPTER 2

Missionary Selling

In addition to technology skills, most billion-dollar entrepreneurs started out with sales skills and financial management skills. They were, in essence, technologist-accountants who knew how to sell. They knew how to convert skeptics and nonbelievers in a new venture into believers and customers. They were missionaries who could get converts for their new business.

"Business without sales is like Hamlet without the prince."
—Source Unknown

Missionary sales are crucial for a new venture. At startup, no one knows who you are—and no one cares. For initial sales with attractive prices and high margins, entrepreneurs should understand customers' unmet needs, make them happier than competitors can, and gain a competitive advantage to keep them happier in the long term.

Consider a group of 28 Minnesota billion-dollar and hundred-million-dollar entrepreneurs and the skills they started with (see Table 2).

**TABLE 2. SKILLS OF MINNESOTA'S MOST
SUCCESSFUL ENTREPRENEURS**

	NUMBER	PERCENT
Sales & marketing	23	82
Sales	18	64
Accounting/finance	18	64
Technology	7	25
Marketing	5	17
Management	1	4

Source: Bootstrap to Billions, Dileep Rao, www.uentrepreneurs.com

At the outset, the billion-dollar and hundred-million-dollar entrepreneurs were strongest in sales/marketing (82%) and in financial management (64%), enabling them to sell more with less. These entrepreneurs knew how to sell to offer maximum value for customer happiness, for higher margins and at the least cost, and to dominate with higher cash flow. And they used accounting skills to control their cash and cash flow and do more with less. They were accountants who knew how to sell.

Following are some billion-dollar entrepreneurial skills for missionary sales with attractive margins.

Target the Right Customers

If you spend too much money to find customers—or worse, you spend too much time and money to find the *right* customers—you could fail before you have a chance at success. The key is to know who your customers are and how to reach them most effectively and efficiently.

Don Kotula, the founder of Northern Tool, placed small ads in magazines that his core market read. These magazines included *Popular Mechanics, Popular Science, Farm World* (and other agricultural magazines), and a variety of publications for the construction industry. He tracked the orders and continued to use only the magazines that produced results. He also found that there was seasonality to his sales, so he adjusted and did not waste money in the low months. He developed his own mailing lists from his ads and got customers' addresses from their checks. He would encourage his customers to refer their friends to receive a catalog, and most of them were happy to do so. This helped Kotula to expand his mailing list without a high cost.

Make Customers Happy

Happy customers stick to you. Happy customers pay more. And happy customers tell others how happy they are with you.

Horst Rechelbacher, Aveda Corporation's founder, liked to make people happy. As a young man working in hair salons, he realized he worked better when he did not do styles to satisfy himself but to please the customers. He found that customers were the ultimate teachers and that people could tell you what they liked *after they saw it, felt it, touched it, heard it, or smelled it* (he believed in using the senses for selling). If he did something for himself without his customers' approval, his problems and complaints increased. So he would show them photos of various styles, hair lengths, or colors that he was thinking of, and he obtained their feedback to find out what they liked and did not like before cutting and styling their hair. With these skills, he was winning hairstyling competitions in Austria and Europe starting at the age of 14. That was the foundation for Aveda.

Find the Hook for Missionary Sales

The keys to obtaining a competitive advantage and increasing sales are quite simple: Get close to your customers and know how to make them happier.

To generate sales for her fledgling ViroMed company, Bonnie Baskin thought she needed an angle so that customers, who were pathologists, would work with her. She offered a special courier service to pick up samples from the hospitals for testing. And since a virus often dies between the time of pickup at the hospital and delivery to the lab, Baskin equipped a van as a lab to keep the viruses alive. Baskin herself became the first courier so that she could meet more customers, know their needs, offer great customer service, make sure the samples were handled with care, and save money. This strategy succeeded, and customers started working with her.

Gain Credibility and Trust

Technologists often believe that all they need to do is to build a product they think is great, and it will sell itself. Unless you are incredibly lucky, that never happens. Every business needs to understand how to sell its products and the company, most efficiently. You need to seek the right potential customers and then convince them that you can solve their unmet needs. Credibility and trust are the key ingredients when it comes to missionary selling of revolutionary products. To gain credibility and trust, you will also need to find the best sales driver, and find it before you go broke.

As Medtronic, the developer of cardiac pacemakers, started to market its products, they tried a variety of sales drivers such as distributors, reps, internal sales personnel, and trade shows. Since the pacemaker was a revolutionary technology, physicians did not always know what the product was or what it could do, so they did not know how their needs could be met. At the outset, Earl Bakken and his partner found that it was not easy to convince the conservative medical establishment to use their pacemakers. Physicians would even try to avoid them at surgical conferences. However, when leading physicians presented their groundbreaking advances with Medtronic pacemakers at surgical conferences, other physicians would start to use their products. Medtronic started to receive worldwide attention and orders. Physicians listened to leaders in their own profession, but not to entrepreneurs trying to "sell" them a product.

Find and Use the Best Sales Driver

One of the most difficult tasks is to find the right way to sell. Finding the right sales driver can help make sales faster and with less investment. Not finding the right sales driver could mean failure. But each venture needs to find the best way for itself. This means that entrepreneurs need to have the skills to find the best sales driver. A great sales driver helps customers understand the product or service, and the benefits.

Dick Schulze, founder of Best Buy, decided to become a sales rep in consumer electronics because his dad was also a sales rep (in industrial electronics). Schulze was representing leading-edge consumer electronics companies such as Sony at the dawn of the consumer-electronics age. As a sales rep, he learned what it takes to succeed in retail, including how various offers and pricing affected consumers, how to train and compensate sales personnel, how to merchandise and set up floor displays, and how competitors priced their products. This experience as a sales rep taught him more about the retailers' business than the retailers knew themselves. He also learned that many of the retailers were electronics hobbyists but not sophisticated retailers.

After five years as a rep, he became an audio-products retailer and ended up competing with some of his old customers. They did not like it. He learned how to help the customer put together the best package easily and effectively, to offer more features, and to allow consumers to evaluate components with an easily understood floor demonstration so that they could spend less money getting the right sound for them. *The other retailers loved the sound of sound. Schulze loved the business of sound.*

Find the Right Media

There are many ways to sell. Find the way to get the most high-margin sales in the least time with the lowest cost for the happiest customers. *Know the effectiveness of your sales drivers.* Know the return from each ad and each dollar spent on sales drivers. Cut the poor ones. Focus your resources on the ones that work. Gather competitive intelligence. Check with people who sell to competitors. Sales people are "great gossipers," noted Guy Schoenecker, who founded Business Incentives, a $500 million corporation.

Schoenecker started by opening a furniture store. He did not advertise in the major newspapers because he found that his ads did not draw enough business to pay for the cost of such advertising. He checked with friends who were in the media industry and sold advertising to some large furniture retailers, and he learned that their ads in the newspapers were hit-and-miss, with some ads doing well and others failing. Schoenecker could not afford to gamble, so he focused on the sales driver that worked for him, which was direct mail. He developed a monthly direct-mail flyer. This would generate business for the first two weeks of each month, and he would deliver the items in the last two weeks.

Ed Flaherty (Rapid Oil Change) did not know the right way to promote his quick oil-change service to attract the type of customer he wanted. So he tested a variety of media to see what worked and what did not. He realized that he needed two kinds of promotion. He needed to build his brand throughout the metro area so that customers would learn of his business and feel comfortable using his services. Brand building also attracted the higher-margin customer. He achieved this objective through mass media such as TV and radio. However, to attract traffic to each store, he needed to conduct neighborhood-targeted marketing, and this he did with direct mail, door-to-door coupons, and advertising in the local newspaper. He measured his investment and the sales and margin returns from each media investment, eliminating ones that did not work and enhancing those that did.

When he was fourteen, Don Kotula (Northern Tool) was working for his dad and got his permission to try advertising to expand his territory. However, his dad wanted Kotula to show that each dollar spent on advertising paid for itself, produced additional marginal sales, and was profitable. Kotula advertised in the local and regional shoppers (newspapers that were popular before the days of Craigslist) and other media, such as national construction magazines, to see what worked and what did not. He tracked each ad to see how it did, because he had to prove to his dad that he was not wasting money. The company's market, sales, and profits expanded significantly.

Communicate the Benefits

It is tough to sell, and especially to sell value, unless you know the value of your product to your customers and can communicate the benefits to your customers by making it "instantly intuitive." Communicate the benefits immediately if you want to grab customers' attention. If they don't understand the benefits, they don't buy or pay high margins.

When Lloyd Sigel (Lloyd's Barbeque) was getting started, ribs were not a high-demand cut of meat, and Armour (his first full-time employer) could not sell its raw ribs at profitable prices. Armour also had a substantial canned ham business, and one of its ideas was to sell barbecued ribs in a can. This led to a new idea for a product called "cooked ribs in a tin." However, salespeople at Armour had been unsuccessful at selling this. Sigel did some research and realized that the consumer did not understand the product. He took about 25 empty tins with labels, built a faux, portable barbecue pit with brick facing, placed the can in the middle on a pole, and added a motor to rotate the pole—to convey a rotisserie image of meat that had been cooked. This gave a visual picture about the product. The product sold.

Merchandising

Entrepreneurs need to know how to merchandise, whether the business is in-store or online. This means that you need to find the needs, unmet or otherwise, of your customers and be able to sell them the products and services that will make them happy. When I managed a chain of fast-food stores, I found that one of the most crucial questions you can ask is, "Do you want fries with that?" Many customers do, but they need to be asked. And fries are one of the most profitable items in a fast-food store. Now that much of retail has moved online, you need to know how to merchandise online.

One of Jeff Bezos's key innovations at Amazon.com was the online recommendation engine. The recommendation engine was Amazon's equivalent of a clothier selling ties, shirts, and shoes with a new suit. By understanding the customer's likes and dislikes, Amazon could make new recommendations the customer was expected to like.[1]

Presentation

Impressions matter. It is amazing that buyers are impressed with form rather than substance, but that is how many customers buy. Understand not only your competitive advantage but also how to attract buyers and have them take you seriously.

Tim Doherty built his company, Doherty Employment, to over $400 million in revenues. One of his first corporate customers asked for a formal proposal, after which Doherty was not selected. The vendor who was selected boasted to Doherty, "You got outsold, kid." But the company could not deliver on its promises, and the client company asked Doherty for help. Doherty asked why he had lost the sale in the earlier round, and he was shown the competitor's sales materials to compare with his own. Doherty's were simple and plain, while the competitor's had lots of razzle-dazzle. Doherty realized that big corporations want impressive-looking sales presentations.

Form the Right Alliance

Alliances can help. The right alliance can open large markets, add credibility to make your product a standard, and help you sell to new customers who may not have heard of you.

Bill Gates made Microsoft the de facto standard for the PC industry by convincing IBM to use his operating system for their computers. Steve Ells also made Chipotle the standard by forming an alliance with McDonald's.

Understand the Retail Process

Understand not only your customers, but the entire retail process—that is, the consumers and the competition. Be prepared, anticipate objections, and understand that the customer nearly always has alternative purchasing options. Put yourself in their shoes and understand their problems. Retailers want to sell more. Suppliers need to offer a better package to help them sell more at attractive prices.

Glenn Hasse started Ryt-Way, a venture based on a new packaging concept to package instant nonfat dry milk and built it into a $100 million-plus corporation. Hasse calculated the number of bags that could be produced with the equipment he was considering using. He assumed that, with a capacity of 400 cases per day, he would make a profit. Hasse expected no problems in selling his entire inventory. So he bought the equipment, hired employees, and started what he thought would be a new, profitable enterprise. However, after selling 2,500 cases, he ran into a brick wall.

To increase sales, Hasse met with a major food distributor who pointed out that food is a percentage business. If they sold some product for $20, they would make two percent, or 40 cents. If they sold it for $11, as Hasse was proposing, they would only make 22 cents. Since customers were buying the higher-priced product anyway, he asked Hasse, "Why should I buy yours?" He told Hasse that having the lowest price would not get the channels excited. Hasse needed to understand the retail chain.

Adjust to the Slow Pace of Missionary Sales

Sales at the start are usually slow. Sales grow more rapidly after the market has accepted you and you understand how to sell. That is why in high-growth companies, sales growth takes the shape of a hockey stick.

This is what happened at Tastefully Simple. At her first home taste-testing party, Jill Blashack Strahan's goal was to have 12 people at each party and sell $300 worth of products, for an average sale of $25. She was also expecting one or two people at each party to offer to host additional parties. At her first party, she sold about $200 worth of products to five people (for an average of $40). The attendance was smaller than her goal, but the average sale was higher. Most importantly, four attendees wanted to host parties. But after a promising start, Tastefully Simple's growth started to sputter. Blashack Strahan had to find renewed inspiration and have faith in her product line and sales mission. She redefined her goals, renewed her spirit, and restarted her business. She renewed her spirit by realizing that her problems were minor compared with those of many others. She also went as a corporate guest to Creative Memories' national conference. Creative Memories, a nearby company that sells keepsake albums and supplies, also used a direct sales network. Blashack Strahan was infused with a new sense of optimism, learned new skills, and had new faith in her journey. The company started to grow, and Tastefully Simple expanded to 28,000 sales consultants nationwide.

Sell without Money

Selling to consumers can be quite expensive, primarily due to the cost of selling and marketing, including the cost of promotion, public relations, sales personnel, and building a distribution system to reach and sell to them. This can be a problem, especially at the start, due to a shortage of funds, the high cost of getting more funds, and the cost and time required to attract customers in a new business.

Ken Dahlberg (Dahlberg Electronics) had two products (communications products and hearing aids) and two markets (consumers in hospitals and the hospitals themselves), and he had to find a way to sell both products and do it cheaply. When talking to potential customers, he found that "everyone knew at least 10 people with hearing problems," and they were glad to refer Dahlberg to their friends. By the time he sold the company to Motorola, the hearing-aid division had become a leader in the industry.

· · ·

The most difficult part of a new venture is to learn how to sell high volumes with high margins in the least amount of time and with the least cost—when no one knows your name.

CHAPTER 3

Operating Frugally

It is usually more difficult to be frugal in sales than in operations. Most entrepreneurs seem to have a feel for cutting expenses in operations by renting rather than buying, and outsourcing rather than making. But don't lose the long-term advantage for short-term expediency.

"They liked machinery. I liked customers."
—Glen Taylor, Taylor Corporation

Large, existing companies can afford to hire industrial engineers and operations experts to improve operations and reduce unit costs. But this is usually the result of a large investment in fixed assets.

Entrepreneurs need to rely on themselves to operate to make customers happier, to do it with less money because they don't have access to cheap money, and to make money at the same time. Their unit costs may be higher, which can reduce their gross margins. But strong entrepreneurs add value, so they should be able to charge higher prices and attain reasonable margins.

Following are some billion-dollar entrepreneurial skills for frugal operations to make customers happier while keeping costs lower.

Learn to Jump into an Emerging Industry

Billion-dollar entrepreneurs such as Bill Gates, Steve Jobs, Mark Zuckerberg, and Travis Kalanick entered emerging industries. Because an industry is emerging, no one is experienced, so everyone is experimenting with alternative operations to become more efficient and learn the skills needed to succeed.

Medtronic had growing pains as it led the emerging medical device industry. After the initial success with the pacemaker, Medtronic significantly overextended itself and ran into financial problems. That's when it realized that it had to focus. Medtronic decided to focus on implantable therapeutic technologies (devices) that restored people to meaningful lives. This meant that they would not spend resources in other areas such as diagnostics or laboratory products. This new mission and plan helped Medtronic to focus, bring order and control while keeping its zeal, and grow its sales and profits. Medtronic started to thrive.

Skills and Experience in Existing Industries

Billion-dollar entrepreneurs in more mature industries had significant experience in the emerging industry. This category included Dick Schulze (Best Buy), Steve Ells (Chipotle), and Amancio Ortega (Zara).[1] These entrepreneurs were experienced or trained in their industries and thus could operate frugally while jumping on emerging trends.

Dick Schulze learned the nuts and bolts of consumer electronics retailing while working as a sales rep for Sony and others. He learned what it takes to succeed in retail, including how various offers and pricing affect consumers, how to train and compensate the sales personnel, how to merchandise and set up the floor displays, and how competitors priced their products. After five years as a rep, he lost some of his product lines and realized that manufacturers could fire him even if he met all expectations. He wanted to control his own destiny and decided to start his own business. This was the start of Sound of Music, which morphed into Best Buy.

Focus Resources to Beat First Movers

When others are growing without a plan, a focused strategy can target resources to dominate markets.

When the big-store retail concept started emerging, the leaders in the industry were Kmart and Target. Meanwhile, Sam Walton had a small chain of retail stores in rural Arkansas. Seeing that this big-store concept could dominate the industry, Walton jumped in. Noticing that the big companies were focusing on urban America, Walton focused his attention on small towns because the competition there was weaker, and he knew small towns. He started by expanding in the South and then moved on to the rest of the country. He built his own system of warehouses and trucking to supply his stores. His domination of small towns gave him the springboard to expand into urban markets and dominate.

Focus on the Unmet Need

Initially, entrepreneurs don't have resources to waste and the cost of money is high. Focusing on the unmet need can help to attract high-value customers and keep them. To do this, understand customers' real pain. Usually those who are responsible for implementation know the real pain and the importance of solving it. Their futures are at stake.

To better serve their needs, Tim Doherty (Doherty Employment, a temp employment agency) asked employers about their major problems. Some would tell him. Many would not. He found out that this was because the executive decision makers often did not always know the real issues and the real pain. The answer lay with lower-level supervisors who experienced the problems. Doherty started contacting supervisors at the production line or at the supervisory levels before reaching higher up in the corporation. This made his job easier when he approached the top-level managers because he already knew the people who had to implement the program and understood their problems.

As he talked with more companies, Doherty found that his competitors did not adequately serve the needs of the third shift, which had unique issues. The larger-company managers liked to have their evenings and nights free, but that's when the shift supervisors had problems getting help. Doherty took calls at home in the evenings and nights, and he took his files home with him so he could find employees for these companies whenever they had needs. He answered calls until midnight or 12:30 a.m., and he and his wife (and future business partner) called temp employees and often woke them up to offer them work. Doherty found that the national company executives (his competitors) were oblivious to the third shift. This focus on the third shift was not a predetermined strategy or the result of market research. He just started getting calls from desperate supervisors who found his name in the yellow pages, and he was often the only temp agency who answered the phone.

Attain Industry-Specific Skills

Every industry has unique needs—and requires unique skills to solve industry-specific problems. In established industries, experience in the industry helps lead to attaining these skills. Or you may need a partner who has them. In emerging industries, you need to have the skills needed in the industry and be a fast learner.

Although Ed Flaherty (Rapid Oil Change) was advertising a 10-minute oil change, each one was taking him 30 minutes. One afternoon, in his store in the Minneapolis suburb of Bloomington, a customer came in and intently studied his operation. Being the friendly sort, Flaherty started chatting with the man, who happened to be an employee of Andy Granatelli, the owner of a famous race car team. This man knew how to change oil and how to do it fast. It turned out that his wife was from Bloomington, he was in town to visit her parents, and he was bored stiff. His first comment to Flaherty was, "You don't know what you're doing, do you?" When Flaherty agreed, the gentleman reorganized the store's layout and helped him reduce the time to change oil from 30 minutes to under seven.

Learn Cost-Control Skills

The early years are usually the toughest. Keep your overhead and administrative costs low, and you can survive even with low levels of sales.

Glenn Hasse (Ryt-Way, a subcontract food packager) knew that price was crucial in his industry. To stay competitive, he excelled at cost control. When he landed a major contract with Hormel, he designed and built the equipment himself. As his experience grew, he improved the automation of the equipment and fine-tuned its efficiency. In the first 10 years, he was the general manager, operations manager, and sales manager; when the plant was busy, he was managing the work. Whenever the plant operations slowed down, he would solicit business.

Raise Productivity

Whether you are in an emerging industry or an established one, productivity is always crucial. You need to raise value to achieve higher prices and margins, but you need to cut costs by increasing productivity for improved cash flow. To improve productivity, you need to know what to expect, and then organize to make your operations more efficient and achieve more. You also need to act when your standards are not met and to reward employees based on their productivity and contribution to the company. Make sure you are fair. Word gets around.

To increase productivity, billion-dollar entrepreneur Glen Taylor (Taylor Corporation, the wedding invitation printer) set out to develop standards for employees and the plant's machines—and then improved on them. He analyzed all his operations and then simplified them to gain efficiencies. He monitored all his divisions and their key components every day, including orders, shipments, and production. He instituted information systems even before the prevalence of computers by developing a card system to keep track of the key data he needed.

All supervisors had to know the productivity for each of the people they managed at the end of each day. Taylor instituted four pay scales (A/B/C/D) based on production. Employees started at the lowest scale and were promoted to higher pay scales as their productivity improved. Taylor based pay scales on productivity, rather than on time served. If employees could not maintain their productivity, the supervisor would assist them. If they needed a slower pace, they were moved to another job at a lower scale. Production employees were offered a profit-sharing system tied to their individual companies (not to the parent Taylor Corporation), along with a pension fund and a 401(k).

Motivate Employees without Shortchanging the Customer

It's important to structure incentive packages intelligently. *People work for themselves*. If you are fair with employees and offer them a fair share of the profits, they will work harder for you. But make sure you develop a fair system and don't offer incentives that could shortchange your customer.

To make sure that everyone was working toward the same goal, Flaherty set up an incentive system at Rapid Oil. Everyone in the store received a percentage of store profits. He split his operating income with managers, assistants, and employees. Flaherty found that some managers turned customers away before closing time to clean the store so they could finish at the closing time. Flaherty added a $1-incentive per car after a certain number of cars were serviced during the day. He also offered a share of sales from parts. However, to prevent his employees from selling parts that customers did not need, the employees did not receive any percentage if the parts sales exceeded a certain percentage of store sales. He did not want greed to affect customer satisfaction. Flaherty also believed in giving his existing employees first shot at any managerial positions, if they were outstanding employees and had the right attitudes. This motivated them to work harder.

Benchmark and Add Value

Start by examining how the others in your industry perform and succeed, and analyze how you can differentiate yourself based on customers' unmet needs to add value.

Glen Taylor compared his wedding-invitation catalog with those of the leaders in the industry. And he asked himself a simple question: Why would people buy from him? He could not see an obvious advantage, and he concluded that many customers were buying from his company because they were local customers and he charged less. To improve his margins, he developed a fancy, rich-looking catalog that imitated competitors' designs and included all the most popular products. On items that were easy to compare, he set prices slightly below the competitors', giving customers a reason to buy from him; but he sought higher prices on accompanying items and customized options. Sales and profits started to increase.

Hire Right

Human resources are a key asset in any business, especially in new ventures. Entrepreneurs need to constantly worry about recruiting the right quality and quantity of employees needed, to continuously upgrade and retain the ones they want, and eliminate the ones who are not beneficial to the company.

To find excellent store managers, Ed Flaherty studied the job requirements for managers at his Rapid Oil locations and realized that he needed people who liked fast-paced work. Flaherty found that the fast-food industry trained its managers to supervise people, equipment, and operations to provide a high quality product (that is, as much quality as fast food can deliver) and service. These managers needed to know "time compression," that is, how to deliver this high level of service in a fast-paced environment. Also, the fast-food industry paid its store managers well but was not as generous with its assistant managers. Since the fast-food industry was starting to slow down from its torrid rate of growth, the assistant store managers were no longer finding as many challenging opportunities for growth and promotion—and were facing a dead end. Flaherty had a new store manager who had been an assistant manager at a fast-food store, who pointed out to him that the pace at his new job was just as fast, challenging, and fun as his old job in fast food, but it was more profitable. This manager also knew many fast-food assistant managers who were anxious to make their mark and eager to jump into a hot new company that valued their skills more. Flaherty started recruiting from the fast-food industry.

Continuously Improve in Areas Valued by Customers

If one side of the coin is to make customers happier, the other side is to do it with the highest productivity. By making customers happier, entrepreneurs can keep them and command a higher price due to higher value. By being more productive, costs are lower and profits are higher.

Bob Kierlin built Fastenal, a seller of nuts and bolts, into the largest fastener company in the U.S. and one of the largest in the world. At the outset, Kierlin raised $31,000 from his own savings and financing from a few of his friends. He calibrated Fastenal and realized that the most important numbers were inventory turns and gross margins—if he wanted to grow with internal cash flow. That is what he controlled, and his company eventually became a consistently high-performing publicly traded corporation.

Keep Secrets

When you are ahead of the industry, stay quiet. *Don't boast about what you have learned.*

Fastenal's Bob Kierlin and his key team were self-trained in improving their productivity. Since they had not gained much from the industry, they did not see the need to share what they had learned with the rest of the industry. They decided that the best strategy for them was to continuously improve on their own and to avoid sharing these strategies with the industry. Others tried to steal their employees, but these companies did not have the right environment to profit from Kierlin's improvements.

• • •

To improve productivity frugally, you need to know what to expect, and then organize to make your operations more efficient. Reward employees based on their productivity and contribution to the company. Make sure you are fair. Building a business is not all glamour and talking to the media. Most of it can be termed "boring" routine, but it needs to be done, and done frugally and effectively.

If you select outsourcing to launch your venture, be careful that you don't expose yourself to the risk of losing your intellectual property. Entrepreneurs have often lost their edge by outsourcing to companies that appropriate the technology.

CHAPTER 4

Revolutionary Visioning

A new industry, or an existing industry that is being impacted by a revolutionary trend, is chaotic. Highly successful entrepreneurs see through the chaos, noise, and clutter of a new, emerging industry or the patterns of change in a fragmented industry, and find the right opportunity and strategy to dominate it. That is the essence of revolutionary visioning.

"I would rather gamble on our vision than make a 'me, too' product."
—Steve Jobs

Billion-dollar entrepreneurs are revolutionary visionaries. They dominate fragmented industries that have no leaders, or they take a lead and never relinquish it in high-potential, emerging industries created by revolutionary technologies and trends.

To dominate the industry, billion-dollar entrepreneurs find the fulcrum and develop the strategy to become the first dominator, not the first mover. They do so by developing skills in emerging industries; by evaluating the trends and gauging the potential; by understanding the value that can be offered to the right customer segment; by evaluating the competition; and then by developing the strategy to find the edge for long-term dominance.

With skills and expertise in emerging trends or technologies, billion-dollar entrepreneurs find a way to put it all together and dominate. Here are some of their skills.

Visioning Skills for the Right Track

The growth tracks used by billion-dollar entrepreneurs are shown in Figure 1.

CAPITAL INTENSITY (CI)

Capital-intensive ventures expect the industry to grow rapidly and seek to spend large amounts of capital to dominate it. These expenses and investments are made ahead of revenues, causing losses and negative cash flow. This negative cash flow is hopefully funded by angel capitalists and VCs.

After Pierre Omidyar started eBay, sales began growing rapidly. This attracted better-funded ventures in the same space, causing Omidyar to get VC before he could prove his personal leadership potential. He was replaced by Meg Whitman.

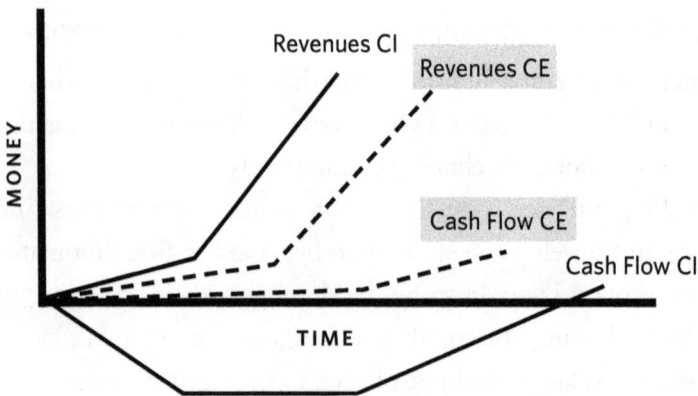

Figure 1. Capital efficiency (CE) vs. capital intensity (CI)

CAPITAL EFFICIENCY (CE)

Capital-efficient ventures grow slower at the start, yet this approach can enable the venture to break even financially or have positive cash flow, even if in small amounts. It may take longer to reach takeoff.

Finance-smart entrepreneurs accept external financing that lets them retain control of their venture. This means that they use alternatives to VC so long as VCs seek to control the venture and recruit a professional CEO. When the entrepreneurs reach the point where they can get VC and stay on as CEO, they may feel more amenable to VC. The result is that their growth rate may be lower before they accept VC and higher after they get it.

Steve Ells started Chipotle with his family's help. When they reached the limits of their own and their network's financial capacity, Ells obtained strategic financing from McDonald's and continued to lead his company to dominate the industry.

HYBRID

Hybrid ventures are the third track, combining the capital-efficient and the capital-intensive. Hybrids are capital-efficient until Aha. After Aha, they seek VC for a competitive advantage and to grow faster to dominate the industry.

Many famous entrepreneurs such as Bill Gates (Microsoft), Jeff Bezos (Amazon.com),[1] and Mark Zuckerberg (Facebook) started their ventures with their own savings or with funding from family, friends, and angels. After proving their leadership capacity, they got VC and stayed on as CEO.

The choice for you is to choose between capital intensity, capital efficiency, or a hybrid growth track. To grow with control, entrepreneurs need skills to grow without capital until Aha. At Aha, the world can see your potential, which gives you more choices to find the right VC funding or grow without VC.

Visioning Skills by Stage

Successful corporate executives manage to find an edge in slow-moving businesses in mature industries. Finance-smart entrepreneurs, however, need the right skills to develop potentially successful strategies at each stage of a fast-changing emerging industry, and they need to succeed in the subsequent stages to dominate. The key stages for entrepreneurs are research and development, launch, and growth.

RESEARCH AND DEVELOPMENT (R&D)

At the R&D stage, entrepreneurs need the right skills to know what type of product or service they need to develop to succeed. These skills entail understanding the capabilities and limitations of leading technologies that affect the product or service, and the key unmet needs of the best segment that is most likely to switch to the new offering. In many cases, this may have to be done in the dark, so to speak, because the strategies of other companies—established or emerging—may not be known.

Steve Jobs was a master at this stage. He was able to evaluate the strengths and weaknesses of the first movers and develop iconic products such as the iPod, the iPhone, and the iPad to dominate their respective emerging industries.

LAUNCH

After developing the product or service, entrepreneurs need to know how to envision the right strategy to launch the venture and take off with the limited resources they are able to muster. This means you need to start with your decision about the most appropriate (for the company) combination of product/service and segment to make customers happier with you than with your competitors for the long term. You also need to acquire skills to launch with limited resources; control expenses in real time; monitor revenues and customer happiness; evaluate competitors and their strategies, advantages, and disadvantages; and juggle all these pieces while taking off before you run out of cash or can raise more cash.

Travis Kalanick changed Uber from a limo service venture to a taxi-less cab business to launch a billion-dollar company—and, in the process, has changed the nature of urban transportation.[2]

GROWTH

After a successful launch, entrepreneurs need to know how to switch from venture mode to corporation mode. This means learning control skills to protect resources, organization skills to build a more productive organization and achieve goals, and leadership skills to dominate the emerging industry.

This is the stage that separates the pretenders from the best. Successful billion-dollar entrepreneurs know themselves, their skills and limits, and the needs of the organization to obtain or learn the right combination of strengths while avoiding weaknesses to build a large corporation and dominate. Jeff Bezos, Mark Zuckerberg, and Bill Gates are great examples of great leaders—sometimes on their own and sometimes with COOs such as Facebook's Sheryl Sandberg.

Successful entrepreneurs first envision how they will beat their direct competitors to dominate their emerging industry, then use any advantage they have in their new technology or trend to beat their giant indirect competitors.

This is how Gates first dominated the PC world and then the computing world. And how Bezos dominated online sales before dominating retail.

Visioning Skills for the Right Direction

Finance-smart entrepreneurs pivot when they see the reality of the market and assess their competitive advantage. In the capital-efficient and hybrid growth tracks, entrepreneurs learn the skills to develop their business. They don't seek controlling capital until their strategy is proven and their potential is evident. To find the right strategy, entrepreneurs may have to pivot, since finding the right strategy on the first try is unlikely when an industry is emerging. By delaying or avoiding VC, they will have the freedom and control to pivot. Figure 2 shows the capital-intensive process and the capital-efficient process. In the capital-intensive process, entrepreneurs seek capital for an unproven business after developing their plan. In a capital-efficient process, entrepreneurs test their plan in the market. They pivot when they find the real advantage and the fulcrum to dominate their industry. They seek VC if needed, only after they take off. By delaying VC, finance-smart entrepreneurs using the capital-efficient process stay in control.

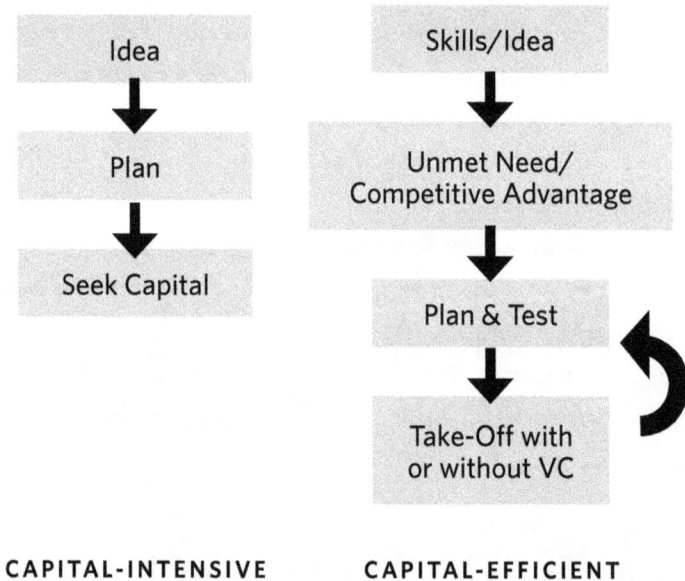

Idea

↓

Plan

↓

Seek Capital

Skills/Idea

↓

Unmet Need/
Competitive Advantage

↓

Plan & Test

↓

Take-Off with
or without VC

CAPITAL-INTENSIVE   **CAPITAL-EFFICIENT**

Figure 2. Capital-intensive process vs. capital-efficient process

Bill Gates did two pivots to build Microsoft.[3] The first was when he found that IBM was seeking an operating system for PCs. He pivoted from writing software to selling the operating system that he bought. His second pivot was when the Internet emerged and Netscape started gaining prominence. Gates changed his operating system to incorporate the web and built a giant.

Jobs did a classic pivot when he returned to save Apple from disaster. Rather than continuing to sell obsolete personal computers, Jobs cut the product line and focused his efforts on the iPod. The rest, as the cliché goes, is history.

Dick Schulze (Best Buy) started his first Sound of Music store when the consumer electronics industry was emerging, and it grew to eight company-owned stores and three franchises. When interstate shipments of products became legal, he realized that he needed to pivot to a big-box store format to compete. This was the right pivot, since he ended up dominating the big-box consumer electronics industry.

Visioning Skills to Put It Together and Dominate

Billion-dollar entrepreneurs had the ability to evaluate the competitive landscape, the potential impact of emerging trends, and customers' unmet needs and then design their unique strategy to dominate. They put it all together by evaluating each building block of the venture and then linking the blocks to optimize cash flow or valuation, avoiding weakness in any block, and dominating with the right one.

Figure 3 shows the building blocks to link finance to the business.

Financial ←→ Launch

Strategy

Finance Smart ←→ Leadership

Opportunity

Control ←→ Organize

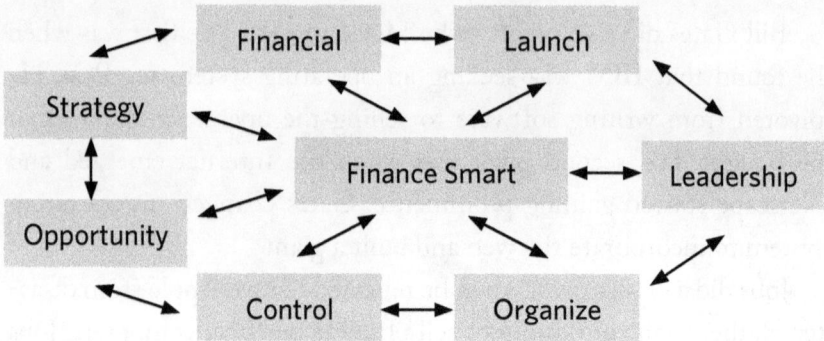

Figure 3. Linking finance to the business

OPPORTUNITY

What will you sell? Do you have an advantage in your product or service that cannot be easily imitated?

Larry Page and Sergey Brin (Google) dominated Internet searching by developing a better search engine that surveyed the entire web and then finding an objective way to rank websites in terms of their popularity by counting incoming links. Others could not catch up.

Earl Bakken (Medtronic) built a company that has dominated electronic medical technology by developing the first cardiac pacemaker because a surgeon wanted a pacemaker that was powered by batteries and not dependent on the electric grid. The company never gave up its lead in the medical device industry.

Many entrepreneurs developed companies to challenge Microsoft's dominance in the PC world. Bill Gates used his control of the dominant PC operating system to develop the Microsoft Office package via acquisitions and internal development to make Microsoft a behemoth.

STRATEGY

At its core, strategy is about what you sell, your target market segment, your direct and indirect competitors, and your competitive advantage.

All of this comes into play if you are to develop a strategy to succeed and dominate. Can you beat your direct and indirect competitors and dominate your market for the long term?

Sam Walton (Walmart) and Bill Gates (Microsoft) have been noted as two of the best examples of using the right strategy for long-term advantage. Walton focused on the rural market for his big-box stores, and this near-monopoly has given him the corporate advantage to dominate the world of retail. Gates used his near-monopolistic profits from his control of the PC operating system to expand into all aspects of the PC world, and then the Internet world.

Jeff Bezos is dominating the business world by helping other companies run their web services, while selling products that often compete with them. Considering that his larger retail competitors, such as Target, helped give him a competitive advantage by using Amazon's web services business, Bezos's strategy can only be considered brilliant.

FINANCING

How will you fund your needs? How can you avoid relying on expensive and controlling financial sources? How can you find sources that are less dilutive and less controlling? How can you find sources that allow you to grow at the right rate?

Richard Burke found financing from a chain of hospitals to perfect his business model, and then from physicians to start UnitedHealthcare (UNH). He started UNH as a manager of health maintenance organizations (HMOs) that were owned by local physicians. After organizing many HMOs, he went public and used these funds to buy the HMOs.

Michael Bloomberg used funding from his own savings and from Merrill Lynch to start his iconic company. Merrill Lynch was a strategic partner and a key customer, but Bloomberg controlled the company.

Dick Schulze got financing from his vendors for his inventory and from lessors for fixed assets to build Best Buy, even though he did not have any equity. He then controlled his business growth and cash flow to make sure he had the cash to meet his obligations.

TAKEOFF

How do you launch and take off with limited cash? How can you juggle all the pieces of your venture in real time, including sales and marketing, monitoring, internal cash flow, and external financing?

Bob Kierlin built Fastenal into a nuts-and-bolts powerhouse by linking his income statement, balance sheet, cash flow, and business strategy. He found that he could grow at 30 percent per year from internal cash flow if he kept his gross margins and inventory turns high and trained enough new managers each year.

Michael Dell built his company by customizing PCs for his customers. He asked them to send their payment along with their order. By getting his customers to pay him up front, he had his working capital. He added to this working capital by getting credit from his vendors.

CONTROL

How can you control the business as it grows? Can you stay in touch on a timely basis with all of the business's many facets, especially as the venture grows beyond a few employees? Are you getting the information in a format that is usable when you need to take action? And does it help you decide what action to take?

Don Kotula knew how to control Northern Tool with the right data. He examined relevant data on a daily, weekly, and monthly basis and used this information to know where to spend his time.

Joel Ronning built Digital River to sell software over the Internet using his encryption software. One of his practices was to get sales figures on an hourly basis from his global offices. On 9/11, he knew within the hour that business was coming to a standstill and adjusted his operations accordingly.

ORGANIZE

How can you transform a venture into a corporation? As the venture grows, do you know how to hire the right people, train them, promote them, motivate them, reward them, and build an organization to dominate?

Dick Schulze built Best Buy by finding the right people, especially in sales, and then motivating them for high performance. He recruited employees based on their sales skills and promoted them based on their achievements and their suggestions for improvement.

After organizing his HMOs, Richard Burke (UnitedHealthcare) had to make sure that all payments and levels of service were reasonable for each type of physician. Often, the representatives on the board had to decide to cut the level of payment to the physicians to keep the HMO solvent, and then go back to their constituents (the same physicians) and explain their actions. It took a lot of courage, and they were not even paid for their time and trouble. It was a thankless job. Burke realized that one of the key requirements for a successful HMO was to find good people to serve on the board and take abuse (without pay) for the good of the physician community. They were physicians who knew that the status quo was not viable because they were losing patients, and they had to control costs. He structured his organization to find and nurture good people, encourage them to sit on the boards, and help them to make the hard decisions. When someone wanted to wait before cutting expenses and payments (and this is frequently the case in turnarounds), he pointed out to them that they could not afford to wait because the consequence of inaction was failure.

Burke realized that he had to develop the culture he wanted. Initially Burke "hired people like himself," and he knew all the employees. He rewarded what he thought was good behavior and successful results. But when he started buying other companies, he realized the importance of knowing what to expect from his expanding staff. He first noted this when he completed his first acquisition. One of the acquired company's managers told Burke that they celebrated failures as a way of learning and also pointed out that it was okay to take risks. Burke only celebrated successes. Burke could also see other signs that the two organizations—and cultures—did not get along. At meetings, Burke wanted a clear agenda, time frames, and a decision at the end of the meeting. At the acquired company, Burke found that they often met for a whole day and the only decision was to meet again. Burke realized that he needed to define and promote the corporate culture he wanted to develop. He decided to create a success-driven culture, where success was rewarded and not failure. He realized that this required finding, training, and promoting good people into the right jobs where they would succeed. He decided what he wanted, put it in writing, promoted it, and monitored to see that the company did it.

Horst Rechelbacher (Aveda) recruited right and trained right. He knew that in the beauty industry, beautiful people sell more. He looked for attractive persons, but he also observed how they interacted with others and how secure they were. He also encouraged them to do a self-introspection to make them more realistic and grounded and to adjust to the "frequency" of the business, that is, the customers and their happiness. He and the team set the goals together, and he wanted the team to "be in front of the goals." He monitored key numbers every day or every week as warranted to make sure that the team and the individuals were performing toward the goals.

Another aspect of skillful organizing is to treat rainmakers (great salespeople) differently from professional managers. Tom Auth built ITI into a leader in the wireless security alarm industry. He realized that rainmakers were driven to show results and needed to be compensated accordingly. Since rainmakers prefer to be paid in commissions when they deliver, he pays them a low base with generous commission programs and no upper limit.

Auth encourages professional builders to work hard and to achieve more since they know that the sky is the limit. With professional managers, Auth pays a higher base and larger bonuses rather than commissions. The bonus is based on both overall company performance and individual performance. Auth also learned that he should be slow to hire and quick to fire. He was able to determine the value of an employee in 30 to 60 days.

LEADERSHIP

How should you grow personally as the venture grows? What are the stages of leadership? How do you develop the skills needed at each stage?

Billion-dollar entrepreneurs such as Jeff Bezos, Mark Zuckerberg, and Steve Jobs grew from founding entrepreneurs to dominant founder-CEOs.

Glen Taylor built an empire in wedding-invitation cards with ownership of more than 80 companies. He recruited hungry managers and then trained them over 18 months. He then motivated them with fantastic incentive programs and made them wealthy, while they made him wealthier.

12 Rules from Billion-Dollar Entrepreneurs to Find Your "It" Factor

How did billion-dollar entrepreneurs find the "it" factor? Here are some examples.

CORNER THE KEYS TO THE KINGDOM—BILL GATES AND MICROSOFT

Bill Gates dropped out of college to join his high school classmate, Paul Allen, to start Microsoft. Initially Microsoft wrote programs for personal computers. When IBM decided to enter the PC industry, they asked Gates to find an operating system for them to license. Gates bought an operating system from a Seattle company and licensed it to IBM for a small one-time fee—but with a non-exclusive agreement. By licensing the operating system to other PC manufacturers, Microsoft has stayed a leader in the industry for over four decades.

The It Factor

While IBM thought it got a great deal by not paying a royalty based on sales, Gates realized that the emerging PC industry needed a standard operating system and that the system that IBM adopted could become this standard, since IBM dominated the computing world at the time. By giving IBM a great deal, while retaining the rights to license the operating system to other manufacturers, Gates made his operating system the industry standard.

CORNER AN ATTRACTIVE MARKET—SAM WALTON AND WALMART

When Sam Walton graduated from the University of Missouri, he opened his first Ben Franklin retail store with his own savings and financing from his father-in-law. Over the years, Walton built a chain of small stores in small towns in Arkansas, Missouri, and Kansas. Then the big-box retail concept emerged with Kmart and Target as early leaders. But Kmart and Target were focused on urban America, based on the assumption that small towns could not support a big-box discount store for long. Sam Walton proved them wrong. His domination of small towns allowed him to use this base to beat Kmart and Target in their urban markets.

The It Factor

To succeed in small-town America, Walton only had to beat the small stores that served this market. To do this, he had to develop his own logistics system, which he did in partnership with J.B. Hunt. Until he saturated and controlled small-town America, he skirted the big cities. When he was done dominating rural America, he expanded to metro areas and destroyed his competition, including Kmart.

DEVELOP THE PLATFORM THAT EVERYONE LOVES TO LOVE— STEVE JOBS AND APPLE

Steve Jobs, Steve Wozniak, and an investor started Apple at the start of the personal computer revolution. They built Apple with Wozniak's product development skills, Jobs's sales and marketing skills, and funding from angels and VCs. But Jobs was fired from Apple when the Macintosh failed to live up to expectations. When he was in exile, he built Pixar into a giant in the movie industry and sold it to Disney. Meanwhile, Apple was floundering, and Jobs returned to save the company. He saved it all the way to the top of the world by first cutting Apple's bloated product line and then developing the iPod, the iPhone, and the iPad.

The It Factor

Jobs was not a first-mover. He imitated and improved in an emerging technology to lead it. But he imitated and improved better than anyone else. He understood his market and offered convenience and style. He developed platforms around his core products, controlled the ecosystem of all the products and services being sold on Apple's networks, and built one of the world's greatest companies.

FIND THE MARKET THAT MOST DESIRES YOU— MARK ZUCKERBERG AND FACEBOOK

Zuckerberg was a software wizard in high school. When he entered Harvard, he introduced apps to link students with "hot" students and classes. Then he developed Facebook, which enabled Harvard students to link with each other. Soon most of Harvard was on board and then most of the world.

The It Factor

Zuckerberg's key advantage was that he was an expert at programming and was developing new products and apps in various areas. By using the concept for linking via Facebook, Zuckerberg allowed Harvard students to link with each other. This exclusivity separated him from his competitors. He then expanded to Stanford and other universities and then to the world. When Zuckerberg found the right hook for the right audience, Facebook took off.

FIND THE PRICING THAT YOUR BILLION-DOLLAR COMPETITORS CANNOT MATCH—JEFF BEZOS AND AMAZON.COM

Jeff Bezos joined the Internet age when he left his job with a Wall Street firm, D.E. Shaw, and headed west to start Amazon.com. He picked the perfect product for the Internet—books. Books have high margins, and his competitors were large bookstores with fixed costs. Using the emerging Internet and without the fixed costs, Amazon could sell books at competitive prices and high margins that his competitors could not match, due to their fixed-cost stores. As Amazon grew, Bezos developed a strong online infrastructure and sold web services to others, *including competitors*.

The It Factor

Bezos's "it" factor was picking the perfect product to sell at the start. He avoided inventory risk (he could return books), expanded the product list beyond what could be sold in stores, and offered a price advantage that could not be matched by the large store-based competitors due to their fixed costs. Then he reinforced his product advantage with an infrastructure edge and expanded his list of products beyond books. Important to note: He sold his infrastructure services to others, including his key competitors, such as Target. To protect itself, another competitor, Walmart, has recently asked some of its suppliers to avoid using web infrastructure services offered by Amazon.com.[4]

FIND A PROTECTED MARKET THAT CAN BE PICKED APART— GARRETT CAMP/TRAVIS KALANICK AND UBER

Garrett Camp and Travis Kalanick started Uber to rent limos. But they soon realized that they could be the intermediary between private drivers who wanted to make money and passengers who wanted more convenience and lower fares. Uber has made anyone with a car into a cab driver by destroying the old rules about cab licenses.[5]

The It Factor

Camp and Kalanick got "it" when they realized that their app allowed drivers to use their own cars. The fact that these drivers were becoming de facto cab drivers without a cab driver's license did not stop them.

FIND THE TREND THAT IS MADE FOR YOUR SKILLS— STEVE ELLS AND CHIPOTLE

When Steve Ells graduated from culinary school, he wanted to start a high-end restaurant. At his first job at a San Francisco restaurant, Ells noticed the demand for high-quality Mexican food made from fresh ingredients. He used funds from his family to start his first Chipotle store selling high-quality, organic, quick-serve food near the University of Denver. His initial sales were about 10 times his breakeven level.

The It Factor

Ells got "it" when he noticed a market demand for high-quality, organic food at his first job. He took this as proof of an emerging trend, and it led him to assess the real, emerging demand for high-quality, quick-serve food.

DEVELOP YOUR EDGE WITH PEOPLE—BOB KIERLIN AND FASTENAL

Bob Kierlin joined IBM after finishing a Peace Corps stint and getting his MBA. Simultaneously, he started working on his childhood goal of building a vending machine to sell nuts and bolts—fasteners. He rented a storefront in his hometown of Winona, Minnesota, to start his vending machine operation. But he noticed that customers who stopped by inquired about buying fasteners that would not be included in the vending machine. Kierlin abandoned the vending machine idea and opened his first store. Today, his company is the largest fastener company in the U.S.

The It Factor

Kierlin got "it" when he saw the real feedback from his proposed market. He heard the reality of customer demand and changed his business plan.

FIND A WAY TO MAKE CUSTOMERS HAPPIER SO THEY PAY MORE—RICHARD BURKE AND UNITEDHEALTHCARE

Richard Burke, the founder of UnitedHealthcare, was a health insurance analyst and helped to pass legislation to promote health maintenance organizations. Initially, HMOs were small and struggling. Burke built UnitedHealthcare into the leader when he found that he could get his customers, mainly corporations, to pay the higher fees demanded by the physicians in his HMO when consumers could keep their favorite physician. This kept the physicians happy, and they provided starting funding for new HMOs. UnitedHealthcare started

by managing HMOs owned by local medical associations (physicians). Then it went public and bought out the physicians.

The It Factor

Burke's key "it" was the realization that consumers wanted to keep
their physicians, and that employers were willing to pay more to
keep their employees happy. That's what made the UnitedHealthcare model tick. Find what will make customers happier so you can
charge more.

BRING ORDER TO THE UNIVERSE—LARRY PAGE/SERGEY BRIN AND GOOGLE

At the dawn of the Internet age, the number of websites was mush-
rooming exponentially. Many search engines emerged to help customers find the right site. But there was no rationale to the system
used to rank and display the search results, and users did not know
which search engines offered the best search results. Page and Brin
realized that a key to ranking the sites was the popularity of the site.
And the key to determine the popularity on an unbiased basis was
to count the incoming links to each site. But to find the number of
incoming links to any site, Google had to survey the entire web and
rank the search results based on popularity.

The It Factor

Google got "it" when Page and Brin realized that the best ranking system was based on the number of incoming links and that
they needed to survey the entire web to do this. It was an unbiased,
rational method for ranking Internet search results. Google crushed
the others.

USE LEADING-EDGE TECHNOLOGY TO DEVELOP HIGH-NEED PRODUCTS—EARL BAKKEN AND MEDTRONIC

After getting a master's degree in engineering, Earl Bakken started his company to fix medical equipment. One day, there was a temporary loss of power. Children who were patients at the University of Minnesota hospitals died when the machine that was keeping them alive stopped. Dr. C. Walton Lillehei, the physician in charge, asked Bakken to develop equipment that did not need to be connected to the central power grid to work. Without a budget, Bakken developed the first cardiac pacemaker in six weeks. To do this, he imitated the circuit for a metronome. That was the start of Medtronic and the electronic medical industry.

The It Factor

Bakken got "it" when he realized that the circuit of a cardiac pacemaker could be the same as that of a metronome. Both went tick-tock. He used a circuit from *Popular Electronics* magazine to start a multibillion-dollar company that saves lives.

USE YOUR PASSION IN AN EMERGING TREND— RICHARD SCHULZE AND BEST BUY

Dick Schulze built Best Buy into the giant of the consumer electronics industry. He started as a sales rep for Sony and other consumer electronics organizations when the industry was emerging. His job required him to help his store-owner customers to merchandise the products, develop the advertising, and train the people to sell. When he lost a key account, and he realized that the retailers were more hobbyists than entrepreneurs, Schulze started his own company and led it to the top of the industry.

The It Factor

Dick Schulze got his technical expertise by fixing car radios in high school. And he acquired sales and merchandising expertise to sell consumer electronics as a rep for companies such as Sony. Schulze got "it" when he realized that he had more skills to succeed than the store owners he was helping.

• • •

In hindsight, the "it" strategy in each of these billion-dollar examples seems perfectly obvious. The problem is making this decision with foresight when industries are emerging and everything looks murky.

Suggestions

How can you find this "it" factor? How do you examine, analyze, and act with foresight to capitalize on what will be obvious to all in hindsight? Here are some suggestions to read an emerging industry or emerging trend:

- Build skills in the emerging technology and target industry.
- Analyze trends and understand their potential impact.
- Know the technology behind the trend.
- Find the unmet need to make customers happier in an under-served segment.
- Study direct and indirect competitors to find their fatal flaw.
- Test various business strategies to find the one that fits your strengths and customer needs.
- Find the *fulcrum* to control the center of the industry.
- When you find it, seek to dominate.

Summary

About 0.02 percent of entrepreneurs can benefit from VC, but these entrepreneurs could benefit more when they get the skills and use the strategies to delay VC. When entrepreneurs can show proof of leadership, they can control the venture and the wealth created.

Bill Gates and Jeff Bezos got VC after takeoff and proof of leadership. They controlled their venture and the wealth created. Mark Zuckerberg started Facebook when he was at Harvard. But when Facebook showed proof of potential by capturing hundreds of thousands of users, he got funding from angels and delayed VC. By delaying VC, he still controls the company.[6]

The remaining 99.98 percent don't benefit from VC. If you are outside Silicon Valley, you should know how to grow without VC. If you are in Silicon Valley, know how to delay VC. To do this, develop finance-smart skills and use finance-smart strategies.

Michael Dell and Michael Bloomberg did not need VC because they developed strategies to grow without it. Bloomberg formed a strategic alliance and received an initial investment from Merrill Lynch,[7] and Dell got an investment from his family. Then they used revenues from customers to dominate their respective industries.

Bob Kierlin built Fastenal into the largest fastener company in the U.S. with $31,000. Dick Schulze built Best Buy with $9,000. Richard Burke built UnitedHealthcare into the world's largest health care management company with a second mortgage on his house and no VC.[8]

To create wealth, control capital—both internal and external. If you need VC, get it after Aha to keep control. Steve Jobs lost control of the company he cofounded, and but for a fortuitous set of circumstances, he would not have had the opportunity to return and build one of the greatest businesses in history.

PART II

INNOVATION FOR MORE POTENTIAL PER DOLLAR

> The basis for all businesses is what they sell. But without a product that has value, you will have a difficult time gaining a competitive edge or high margins for growth with cash flow. But obtaining value is not easy or simple.

How can you find your opportunity for growth—with or without venture capital?

Books, magazines, TV shows, and consultants suggest many strategies to innovate and find growth opportunities. The recommended strategies can include "thinking outside the box," using new technologies developed in research labs, or pursuing your passion to find something innovative. The suggestion to be innovative is especially popular, to find something new, and to become a first mover. Being a first mover is supposed to help you become dominant.

The term "first mover" seems to have a halo around it as a requirement for success. Many entrepreneurs assume that there is an advantage one derives by being the first mover, so they seek to find or develop innovative products or services that have not been sold before. But since most first-mover innovations can be easily imitated and improved, how much is the innovation really worth?

More important, is it smart to be a first mover? Do you have to find something new and unique to succeed? And are there disadvantages to being the first mover?

In fact, there may be a first mover *disadvantage*. Netscape was the first popular web browser. It failed. Other first movers included Visicalc, Digital Research, Ampex, and Archie. Table 3 shows some first movers and the ultimate winners.

Contrary to the myth, there does not seem to be a first-mover advantage because fast followers can often profit from the first movers' mistakes. About 50 percent of first movers fail, and only 11 percent dominate their markets.[1] Researchers Peter Golder and Gerard Tellis found that innovators got only 7 percent of the market. First movers need to spend time and money to educate customers, to convince them they have a need for the new product or service, and to get them to buy. This is not easy. The ultimate winners often learned from the first movers' mistakes and shortcomings, used this information to improve their own product or strategy, and won.

TABLE 3. FIRST MOVERS AND ULTIMATE WINNERS

FIRST MOVERS	ULTIMATE WINNERS
Visicalc (spreadsheet)	Excel (Gates)
Digital Research (PC OS)	DOS (Gates)
Netscape (browser)	Explorer (Gates), Google (Page/Brin)
Ampex (music recorders)	Apple iPod (Jobs)
Many tablet computers	Apple iPad (Jobs)
Archie, WAIS, Gopher (search)	Google (Page/Brin)
Many social networking sites	Facebook (Zuckerberg)

Bill Gates became rich by making the PC operating system the standard, not by inventing it.[2] Steve Jobs built Apple not by inventing the PC, or music downloads, or cell phones, or tablet PCs, but by perfecting the above under the Apple umbrella. Mark Zuckerberg did not invent social networking. He just mastered it. Eli Broad who cofounded KB Home, a Fortune 500 company, notes that "the second guy can just charge along the path the first guy has marked, avoiding the rough patches where he stumbled."[3]

Amancio Ortega and Rosalia Mera cofounded Zara and changed the apparel industry. They imitated the fashions from the leading design houses of Europe and condensed the time to get them on the streets from six months to two weeks.[4]

The VC style is to seek opportunities that can become billion-dollar ventures. They usually replace the entrepreneurs with professional executives and hope to grow. They succeed in about 19 percent of their ventures, and about 1 percent become home runs.

Entrepreneurs used the following finance-smart strategies to find growth opportunities:

- Jump on an emerging, high-potential trend.

- Use passion to add value.

- Imitate and improve for more bang per buck.

- Move fast and better to beat slow and perfect.

- Improve backward from the unmet need.

- Seek a platform for long-term potential.

- Improve frequently for happier customers.

CHAPTER 5

Innovation VC-Style

VCs and billion-dollar entrepreneurs differ in how they find their opportunities. VCs need Aha, when potential is evident. And they want to finance high-potential opportunities. Here's how they find them.

> "Intellectual property has the shelf life of a banana."
> —**Bill Gates**

VCs Add Rocket Fuel to a Hot Opportunity

VCs are extremely selective. Contrary to the hopes of many entrepreneurs, VCs invest in very few ventures. Of the approximately 600,000 to 700,000 new ventures started each year, VCs invest in about 300 startups. Of the 3 million to 3.5 million ventures less than five years old, VCs invest in about 3,000 to 4,000.[1] This means that the vast majority of ventures never get VC. In fact, most will not even see the inside of a VC office.

Here are a few key VC practices that should convince you that you need to take off without VC.

VCS WAIT FOR AHA

With hundreds of entrepreneurs seeking VC, it is only natural that VCs let the entrepreneurs bring the company to a stage where signs of success and potential are evident, and risk is reduced. This puts the burden of initial success on you, the entrepreneur.

Contrary to their reputation, VCs are not foolish, swashbuckling investors. Most VCs wait for Aha. In the first half of 2015, about 1 percent of VC investment was at the early stage.[2] The following list outlines the various stages of VC funding.

- *Pre-product (also research and development) stage,* when the product is not yet ready for sale. The risk is highest at this stage and the target return (what VCs seek but not what they get most of the time) can go as high as 80 to 100 percent per year.

- *Seed/startup stage,* when the product is ready for launch. At the seed stage, the business plan and management team may not be in place, although they are in place at the startup stage. Since the risk of product development has been eliminated and VCs can evaluate the product, the target return is usually lower, around 60 to 80 percent per year.

- *Emerging stage,* when the venture has sales but may still be losing money. Since the business has customers, the investors' risk is lower, and the target returns fall to around 40 to 60 percent per year.

- *Growth stage,* when the venture has momentum and is profitable. At this stage, the key risk is whether there will be ongoing growth and a profitable exit. Target returns can be as low as 30 to 40 percent per year.

VCs invest huge amounts of money after there is proof of potential. VC investment in companies like Microsoft,[3] Google, eBay, and Facebook was after the ventures showed proof of potential, that is, after Aha.

Of the billion-dollar entrepreneurs in Silicon Valley, about 90 percent used VC. These billion-dollar entrepreneurs dominated high-potential, emerging industries, but they usually entered these industries based on their passion for, and expertise in, the new technology—not because they were promised VC at the start. Some then grew with VC.

Larry Page and Sergey Brin (Google) used their technical skills to develop a better search engine and become a leader in the emerging industry of Internet search. Initially, they used angel capital. After Aha, they used VC to become a giant.

Figure 4 illustrates the common stages of VC funding and where Google and other giants obtained VC. The risk is highest for VCs in the early research and development (R&D) stage and decreases as the venture progresses through the startup, emerging, and growth stages. Little VC is available at the early stages and is quite expensive, if available. Most VCs prefer to invest in later stages, and they invest larger amounts in these stages.

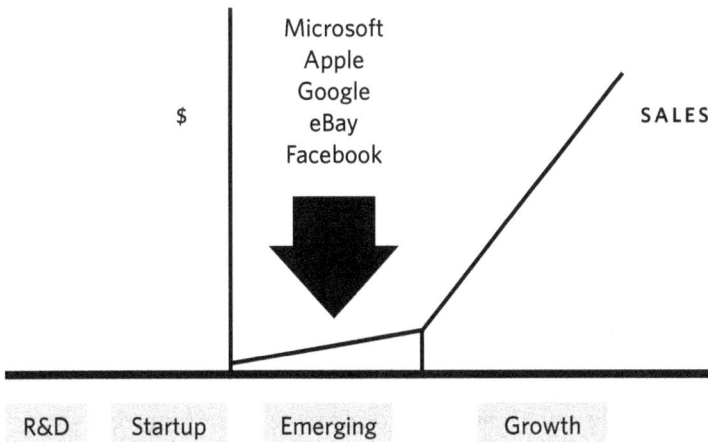

Figure 4. When giants obtained VC

VCS PREFER HIGH-POTENTIAL INDUSTRIES

VCs do best when there is an emerging industry that is creating high-potential opportunities. The last great emerging industries were the Internet 1.0 wave in the mid-1990s and the Internet 2.0 wave of the 2000s. Due to the wide-ranging nature of the Internet, these industries offered many opportunities for VCs, including information search (Google), news (Yahoo), auctions (eBay), products (Amazon. com), and connections (Facebook). When a high-potential industry is emerging, VCs seek ventures that are achieving growth momentum in the industry and can dominate it. Or they jump on technological breakthroughs, such as with Genentech, where one of the cofounders was one of the first to splice the gene. VCs seldom invest in basic research and development due to the high uncertainty and cost and because of the long time periods required and risk to develop a commercially viable product. When they find a viable venture that has momentum in an emerging industry and shows potential to dominate it, they invest.

When there is no emerging industry, VCs often seek ventures that are focused on market niches of established or growing industries. The returns are not as attractive.

VCS PREFER THE EMERGING STAGES OF
HIGH-POTENTIAL INDUSTRIES

Not only do VCs want high-potential industries, but they like to invest in them before dominant leaders have emerged. After dominant companies, like Google, Amazon.com, and Uber, take off in an emerging industry, it is difficult for new ventures to catch up and beat them. It is also easier to grow rapidly in a fast-growing, emerging stage of an industry because you don't have to grab market share from competitors. Most billion-dollar entrepreneurs started their business within three to four years of the start of the industry, when the industry was still in its emerging stages.

VCS PREFER PLATFORMS THAT USE
REVOLUTIONARY TECHNOLOGIES

Revolutionary technologies can create new industries, but those technologies are often developed with government funding. Unlike corporations that prefer evolutionary advances, VCs often prefer products or services that are based on emerging, revolutionary technologies. One reason for this practice is that evolutionary products can be more easily copied by large, existing competitors and can be incorporated into the existing corporate structure, which may hurt new ventures.

VCs mostly invest in ventures that exploit revolutionary technologies that are not easily imitated by large corporations and after the basic research is done. This means that they exploit attractive basic research findings when the industry is emerging. In this emerging stage, the industry is growing and competitors are often newer and weaker. Although the risk is high due to the newness of the industry, the potential and the prospects for growth attract VC investment.

Companies that fit this description include Intel, Google, Yahoo, and eBay. These ventures attracted VC when the industry was emerging.

Unlike VCs, corporations usually prefer to invest in evolutionary products due to the lower risk and compatibility with existing corporate businesses, structures, practices, systems, and channels. Revolutionary technologies can disrupt the corporation's business strategies, markets, and channels. Although there now is greater awareness of the existential dangers to corporations from disruptive innovations and revolutionary technologies, due to the work of researchers such as Clayton Christensen, the problems many corporations face include the high risk to executive careers from high-risk ventures and the potential for cannibalization of existing cash flow. Other hurdles to corporate adoption of revolutionary technologies are the lack of sales history for the products, and uncertainty about the timing for takeoff and the strategy that will succeed.

Financial officers, who have to approve these high-risk investments in emerging industries, reduce near-term risk by avoiding investing in such ventures. But they risk long-term corporate survival, as has been demonstrated by the failure of large retailers like Sears and Montgomery Ward.

VCS INVEST IN A HOT GROUP WITH A COMPETITIVE EDGE

VCs want to invest in a "hot" strategic group that is penetrating new markets in emerging industries with potential for high growth and high valuation.

Within the hot, new industry, VCs like to invest in ventures that have a proven edge and dominate this hot group. Ventures with high levels of proprietary advantages, all other things being equal, are more desirable to VCs than those with limited or no proprietary advantages, due to the potential for greater profitability and wealth creation. VCs also look for proof of potential domination before they invest.

Mark Zuckerberg (Facebook) is a VC-delayer who offered proof of potential domination before getting VC. By using angel capital and waiting until he had momentum, he could pick his financiers and keep control of his venture.

Venture capitalists seek to invest in industries that are taking off and in companies that can dominate those industries.[4] They seek ventures with momentum.

• • •

In the preceding pages we have detailed how VCs want to invest in ventures that have demonstrated momentum and proof of wealth creation. The billion-dollar entrepreneurs profiled in this book, however, avoided VC or grew without it until Aha. The remaining chapters in this section describe how entrepreneurs can find the strategies to do so.

CHAPTER 6

Jump on an Emerging, High-Potential Trend

High-potential trends at an emerging stage are perhaps the most important and greatest wealth generator (and wealth destroyer) in business. To build a giant, high-value venture, find the right trend that you can enter and dominate.

> "You don't have to invent the ocean. Just climb on the right wave. At the right time."
>
> **—Dileep Rao**

To start and develop a high-growth business, find an emerging trend and climb onto it. Emerging trends are often created by changes in business or society, such as the growth of China, and also by new discoveries, such as the Internet.

Using a trend is perhaps the best way to build high-growth businesses. More fortunes are made with a trend than without one, and it is easier for more to grow with a trend than without. If you are an entrepreneur or a corporate business developer, track trends in your industry, in related industries where you can easily expand, in technologies that can affect your industry, and in customer segments that you serve or can serve.

It's important to remember that you don't have to create the trend. Find one and jump on it. Among Minnesota's high-performance entrepreneurs, only 7 percent were trend creators—the rest were trend climbers. Like surfers, they looked for a wave, found one they liked, decided to ride it, and rode it to success.

Entrepreneurs such as Larry Ellison (Oracle), Jeff Bezos (Amazon.com), Bill Gates (Microsoft), and Steve Jobs (Apple) started their businesses by jumping on an emerging industry trend and dominating it. They did not create the trend.

Lloyd Sigel (Lloyd's Barbeque) started his company when more women started working outside the home, and Lloyd's grew with the growing consumer need for refrigerated, cooked meat that could be taken home and heated. Many young women at the time preferred to buy precooked meat because they did not know how to cook raw meat.[1] So cooked meat is what Sigel sold.

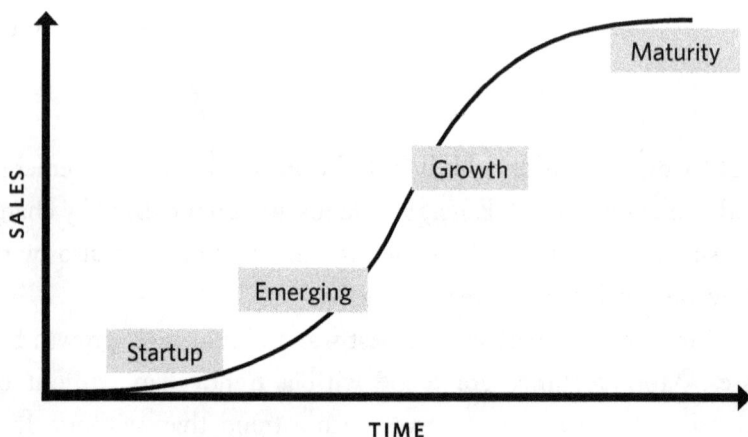

Figure 5. Stages of a cycle

Industries and businesses have life cycles (as you can see in Figure 5). The cycle begins at the startup stage with the creation of the industry or the business, followed by the emerging stage when ventures are seeking the right business model(s) for a competitive edge. Next is the growth stage when the market takes off and the winners emerge and then the maturity stage when growth slows down.

The timing of when the business starts, in relation to the industry trend, can have a major impact on the success and growth of the company. A business that is starting when the industry is emerging, and when all the companies are young, has a better chance to dominate the industry than one that is started when all the companies in the industry are large, established, and successful. At later stages of an industry, new companies need to have a strong competitive advantage to overcome the incumbents' benefits of size, resources, and customer relationships. Alternatively, new ventures may seek a niche market that is not served well by the incumbents.

Craig McCaw and his two brothers bought a cable TV holding company from their father in 1966 and formed McCaw Communications. McCaw studied the industry and found that he could buy licenses for the cellular spectrum (that are needed for cell phones) from the federal government at very low prices. He started buying licenses, used the licenses as collateral to buy more licenses, and sold his cable TV properties to buy even more licenses. When the dominant Bell companies realized what was happening and wanted to own these cellular licenses, McCaw had such a huge portfolio that Bell had to buy from him to build a nationwide network. In 1992, AT&T invested $3.8 billion in return for 33 percent of the company.[2] McCaw sold McCaw Communications to AT&T for over $10 billion. For McCaw, it paid to get in at the right time.[3]

Bill Guthy and Greg Renker built Guthy-Renker from a startup in 1988 to about $1.5 billion in annual sales using infomercials to sell merchandise such as beauty and skin care products and DVDs. They started their business at the dawn of the infomercial age, when the Federal Communications Commission stopped limiting the number of ads in a TV show. At that time, when the industry was emerging, the company could buy a half-hour spot on a channel like Discovery for $50. As the industry has matured and competition has increased, the cost has increased to the $20,000 to $30,000 range.[4]

Importance of Trends

ONLY TWO WAYS TO GROW ORGANICALLY

To grow organically (without acquisitions), you can either take market share from others in a mature industry or you can grow with an expanding industry. Between the two, it is usually easier to grow with an expanding industry than by taking market share from your competitors. Taking market share from competitors requires a competitive advantage, which many may not have, so many often resort to price wars. But price wars can be costly for all parties, and large, dominant, incumbent companies usually win these wars. For most emerging entrepreneurs, the best way to grow is by climbing on an emerging trend and riding the trend to become a big company.

Gustavo Cisneros (cofounder of Univision) noted that one of his rules to build businesses (he has started and developed many to become one of the richest entrepreneurs in Latin America) is to go where the growth is.[5] This allows him to grow with a growing market.

As long as you keep up with competitors and the market, your business can grow with the increased penetration of your emerging industry before you get into the super-competitive battles that erupt when the market becomes mature.

Intel did not create the semiconductor industry, but it dominated the industry as it was emerging. Robert Noyce and Gordon Moore, along with Andy Grove, left Fairchild Semiconductor to start Intel and built it into a powerhouse by taking the semiconductor to the next level by developing the microprocessor.[6] And then they improved it from 2,250 transistors in 1971 to 1.5 billion in 2004.[7]

Microsoft, Apple, and Dell did the same. They all jumped on an emerging trend and grew with it. Then they dominated it.

Growing with a trend was also the main strategy among Minnesota's high-performance entrepreneurs. About 28 percent climbed on a new industry as it was emerging.

When Steve Shank was seeking a new opportunity, he noted that a growing number of adults in America were seeking continuing educational opportunities, that long-distance learning was becoming popular, and that personal computers were becoming ubiquitous. He started Capella University at the confluence of these trends and built a giant. Later, the Internet came along and made this business sweeter. It helps to be fortunate, but you have to be in the arena to be lucky.[8]

Alternatively, find a fragmented industry where entry is easy, and then find a trend to grow. This was the strategy of many entrepreneurs, especially in the food industry, such as Fred DeLuca (Subway), Ray Kroc (McDonald's), and Steve Ells (Chipotle).

GROWING WITH A TREND IS EASIER THAN TAKING MARKET SHARE

Change happens and creates trends. There are many kinds of trends, including technology trends, demand trends, government trends, and so on. Understand trends and learn to take advantage. It is much easier to grow rapidly when one is in a hot trend than without one.

As noted in Table 4, 61 percent of Minnesota's high-performance entrepreneurs entered an emerging market and grew with the industry, while 32 percent were already in the industry and found a trend that was taking off. Ninety-three percent of the entrepreneurs grew with a trend. So unless you are supremely talented and can create the world's next great product, you may want to jump on a wave that is taking off.

**TABLE 4. GROWTH SOURCES FOR MINNESOTA'S
MOST SUCCESSFUL ENTREPRENEURS**

ENTRY	PERCENT
Jumped into an emerging market that grew	61
Entrepreneur was in market; found a trend	32
Created technology and developed market	7

Some of the trends to examine include the following:

- **Economic**—including economic growth, employment rates, wage rates, inflation, taxes, energy costs, productivity, financing, international trade, international competition, etc. Apollo University was started as more adults wanted to earn a degree but were unable to do so because of their full-time jobs.

- **Social**—including urban and rural issues, race, gender, family, pleasure-seeking, leisure pursuits, health, population, education, labor, crime, fads, spending habits, work patterns, language, etc. Starbucks was started as increased numbers of young professionals were seeking a way to pamper themselves without the use of alcoholic drinks and looking for a spot to meet their friends. Chipotle profited from the emergence of the organic food trend.

- **Political**—including international tensions, cartels, government actions, coups, etc. UnitedHealth Group was started as the government sought new ways to manage health-care costs by using health maintenance organizations (HMOs).

- **Technological**—including scientific and technology developments, resources, products, processes, etc. Genentech was started to take advantage of technological advances in gene splicing. In the last 20 years, numerous companies have successfully jumped on the Internet trend.

Riding a trend is one of the common strategies used by billion-dollar entrepreneurs nationwide. The main trends of the last few decades have been caused by new technologies and new markets. And entrepreneurs started companies that became giants in these emerging industries, including Intel (semiconductors), Microsoft (personal computers), Genentech (biotechnology), Cisco (telecommunications), Google (Internet 1.0), and Facebook (Internet 2.0) that grew with the growth of their respective industries.

New business opportunities are also affected by demographic trends, including changes in income, ethnicity, or age. The growth of income in countries such as China, India, and Brazil has created new business opportunities. And in the United States, growing ethnic populations are creating new opportunities for entrepreneurs.

Gustavo Cisneros (Cisneros Group) built Univision into a giant company by climbing on the trend of the growing Hispanic market in the United States.[9]

Major trends also create mini-trends that create entrepreneurial opportunities for smaller, hundred-million-dollar companies.

Steve Shank (Capella) exploited the trend of more people who used long-distance education. Lloyd Sigel exploited the increased demand for precooked meals because more women were working outside the home. He developed and built Lloyd's Barbeque to satisfy the demand.

GROWING WITH A TREND IS EASIER IN FRAGMENTED INDUSTRIES

In fragmented industries, it can be easier to be better than competitors, get more resources, or climb on a trend to gain an advantage. Trends create opportunities and can give you an advantage—if you get in at the right time.

Whole Foods and Chipotle used the healthy eating trend and focused on organic foods in the fragmented restaurant industry.[10]

Walmart took advantage of the trend toward larger stores in the fragmented retail industry, and built an iconic company by developing large stores in small towns.

GROWING WITH A TREND IS EASIER IN NICHE MARKETS

Successful companies have also been built in niche markets of oligopolistic industries to cater to underserved segments without being trampled by giants.

Chobani succeeded in the Greek yogurt niche of the giant food industry by capitalizing on the healthy-eating trend.[11]

Tesla succeeded in battery-powered cars against the world's giant car companies by focusing on the high-income segment that is concerned with the global-warming trend.

• • •

Using trends has been the most frequently used strategy to build giant companies. Find new, emerging trends that are creating new industries, or find trends that are changing existing industries to find your successful opportunity.

CHAPTER 7

Use Your Passion to Add Value

At the start of any venture, or the emergence of any industry, it is never clear when the venture or the industry will take off. After takeoff, everyone wants to enter and share in the feast. But it is often difficult to enter then and beat the ventures with momentum. Passion helps when the prospects and timing are not clear, and passion can motivate you to gain the expertise to dominate it.

> "Aha is that magic moment when the world sees your venture's potential the way you do."
>
> **—Dileep Rao**

Until Aha, the world sees you as wearing rose-colored glasses, and all you have going for you is your passion. Passion is what helps you through the 18-hour days at the stage when potential is not evident, and the future looks dark. Use this passion to advance your opportunity to the point where you and the world are in sync.

Opportunities to start a new business arise from many sources, including using a new technology; perceiving an unmet need and satisfying it; developing a better product or service; copying an existing business in an expanding or new market; climbing onto an emerging trend, industry, or market; relying on new regulations; or following your passion, which can be defined as "what you would do even if there was no money in it." Whether or not you plan to seek VC, developing your passion in a trend helps you to grow. The alternative is to take market share from established competitors (as noted before). This is very difficult unless you have developed a significant advantage that is not easily imitated.

Why Is Passion Important?

Passion helps commitment. Commitment encourages perseverance and the attainment of skills. Perseverance plus skill fosters success.

True passion generates commitment and often breeds excellence. Most of the entrepreneurs I interviewed did not seem to have an advantage at the start. Where is the competitive advantage in selling stereos (Best Buy), or wedding invitations (Taylor Corporation), or nuts and bolts (Fastenal)? Of the entrepreneurs I interviewed, 61 percent started based on their passion, and 96 percent grew with the trends. So find passion, find trends, or find both. As Gary Holmes of CSM Corporation put it, "Don't do it just for the money."

Elon Musk has started Tesla (electric cars) and SpaceX (space exploration). In 2008, Tesla was nearly broke, and the first three rockets from SpaceX were duds. Rather than cutting back, Musk poured the rest of his earned fortune ($75 million) into his company, took over management, and today has $3 billion in contracts for his space company as well as the fastest electric car, with a range of 245 miles from a single charge, which is high compared with the competition. That is the result of commitment, skills, and passion.[1]

MONEY IS SCARCE AND TOUGH TO GET

VC is tough to get in the early stages of a venture. According to PwC MoneyTree data, the range of VC investment at the seed/startup stages has been between 0.32 percent and 1.15 percent between the first quarter of 1995 and 1999 during the Internet bubble, between 0.78 percent in the third quarter of 2002 after the bubble finished exploding, and 1.93 percent in the fourth quarter of 2011. VC is also concentrated, with most of this money available mainly in Silicon Valley. To obtain VC at an early stage, entrepreneurs need to demonstrate an extraordinary advantage in a hot industry.

When John Paul DeJoria was cofounding John Paul Mitchell Systems, he did not have any money, so he slept in his car. The actress Joanna Pettet, who was a friend, offered to rent him a room. DeJoria's phone was answered by an answering machine with Pettet's voice greeting callers. He lived hand-to-mouth for two years, with all his money tied up in inventory.[2]

When Andrew Cherng was still in school in Missouri, he would go to New York to work at a restaurant during his holidays. When his cousin started a restaurant in Hollywood, Cherng worked there before starting his own in 1973 with a $60,000 loan from his cousin and the SBA. The entire family worked there—for free. When Cherng got married, his wife worked for large corporations, so he did not have to take a salary from his business. Nine years later, after more financial security and knowing more about the business, they opened their second store. They learned to manage multiple stores and, in three years, they grew to nine stores. They opened tiny stores with high traffic and revenues. They found great locations on corners for "good daytime traffic and nighttime access." Today, Panda Express has 1,500 stores, with revenues exceeding $1.7 billion. They have little debt, and most stores are company owned.[3]

THE COST OF MONEY IS VERY HIGH

Even if VC were available to you at an early stage, it would be expensive. VCs expect very high returns in the early stages because the risk of failure is high. The return targeted by sophisticated VCs at the R&D stage can be between 80 percent and 100 percent per year to compensate for the high risk. This high target for VC returns is the financial cost to the venture.

THE SOONER THE VC, THE LOWER YOUR WEALTH

Getting VC is not a panacea. VCs demand control. This means that you may not run your business, and you keep a smaller portion of wealth created, if any. The impact of this loss of control and dilution can be huge. Among U.S. billion-dollar entrepreneurs, those who got VC early kept the smallest share of wealth created, while those who avoided VC kept the most. *Wealth kept/created grows as VC involvement falls*, that is, the sooner the VC, the lower your wealth.

TIME TO TAKEOFF IS HAZY

Most revolutionary products and industries do not take off immediately—they require some time. Since it is difficult to forecast the length of time until takeoff, entrepreneurs without passion are likely to quit and miss the ride up.

If you can delay getting funding from angels or VCs, this delay can enhance your wealth and your control of your business. It is usually easier to raise money after your product is ready for sale or you are showing profitable growth in an attractive industry. So *first make* money and *then raise* money to keep control.

Most revolutionary products and industries do not take off immediately. As noted in Figure 6, many new companies share the fate of "Reality B." However, even those who take off, as in "Reality A," do so after an expectations gap.

The best-performing stock in the Russell 1000 during the 1990s and 2000s was Fastenal, which was started by Bob Kierlin in 1967 with $31,000 from friends and his own savings. It took the company 20 years to go public. That is an eternity by VC standards, but a non-VC-funded company like Fastenal could afford to wait.[4]

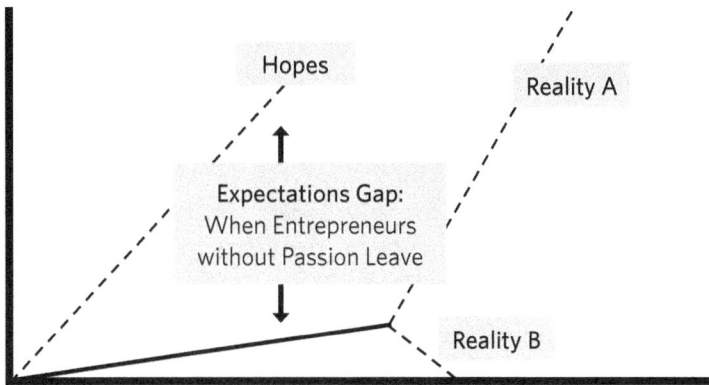

Figure 6. Danger of instant expectations

Fred Smith founded FedEx in 1971 and built it into one of the world's great companies. Smith notes that everything takes longer than anticipated and that most entrepreneurs do not fully understand how difficult it can be to satisfy customer demands and the length of time it takes to do so.[5]

Since it is difficult to forecast the length of time it takes until take-off, entrepreneurs without passion are likely to quit, thereby missing the ride up. Revolutionary products, emerging industries, and new businesses share the same growth curve. They are slow to take off. This means that the length of time to takeoff is unclear, and the venture may have to struggle for a long time. This requires commitment to persist—especially when the present is dark and the future appears darker. Those who expect instant success are likely to leave before it shows up.

Woody Allen was partially right: Success is not just showing up. You have to persist and improve when you are not an instant success.

VCs, however, are not patient. They are evaluated based on the annualized rates of return on their portfolio, and therefore want fast growth from their investments. If the VCs cannot deliver their target returns, they may not survive. So they want ventures that grow fast and create value. Most financiers give up at some point on ventures that they term the "living dead." They reduce their involvement in such ventures due to their high opportunity cost, and the professional managers they attract may also depart to save their careers from an ignominious fate. Entrepreneurs, on the other hand, who have their life and life savings tied up in a venture and who are passionate about what they are doing, prefer not to quit as easily. Without VC, they usually stay and persist. With it, the VCs may sell off any assets to the highest bidder and depart.

Ed Flaherty, who founded the Rapid Oil chain, survived on potato chips and Coke during the lean times rather than seeking VC, which would not have been a likely option since his was not a favored industry for VCs. He eventually sold his company for over $100 million.

• • •

If you have not started your business and are seeking an opportunity, determine your passion and jump on a trend or an emerging industry that can use this passion. While many are searching for innovations, entrepreneurs need to start with their passion and their unique skills, and then they need to find trends.

CHAPTER 8

Imitate and Improve for More Bang per Buck

A prevalent belief is that entrepreneurs need to "think outside the box" and be the "first mover" to succeed. It is ironic that more high-performance entrepreneurs imitated and improved, and were not the first movers. They succeeded because they were more skilled.

> "Success does not go to the first mover.
> It goes to the first dominator."
> **—Dileep Rao**

Billion-dollar entrepreneurs are rarely first movers. They imitate and improve. They make other people's innovations useful to customers—and get more potential per dollar.

Innovation to build successful, high-growth businesses is not just about invention or being the first mover. It is about using inventions to build successful new businesses and to maintain the competitive advantage of existing ones. Invention is only one requirement. Being successful at innovation also requires using the inventions to build new businesses. Harold Evans, author of *They Made America*, noted that "innovation is not simply invention . . . it is inventiveness put to use."[1] Successful innovators need to excel not just at finding or developing inventions or opportunities, but also at building new businesses based on these opportunities.

Why Smart Imitation?

Innovation is expensive. Imitation can be cheaper. Imitation can also succeed when entrepreneurs see weaknesses in the pioneer and find ways to better satisfy customers' unmet needs (see Table 3). But imitation may not be successful if the leader has developed an insurmountable lead, or has developed the perfect product or service that cannot be improved and has strong patent protection, or if many others also imitate and fragment the market.

IMITATION AND IMPROVEMENT WORKS

Imitation and improvement works in emerging industries, and it also works in mature, fragmented industries.

Jim Haslam, who built the Pilot Flying J truck stop and travel center chain, owned a chain of gas stations for cars. Then someone told him about a former University of Tennessee football player who had built a truck stop in Louisiana. Haslam went over, saw it, liked it, and copied it to build one of the largest such chains in the market by offering great customer service.[2]

Imitation and improvement works globally. The practice of imitation and improvement is not only true in Silicon Valley. Some of the world's leading investors practice the same strategy.

In Germany, the Samwer brothers have copied U.S. Internet giants to make a fortune.

Les Wexner of Victoria's Secret and L Brands roams the world to find ideas he can copy and improve.[3]

Gustavo Cisneros (cofounder of Univision and DirecTV in Latin America) became one of the richest entrepreneurs in Latin America by imitating and improving. He did this by looking at what others did in the United States and imitating it in Latin America. When his brother noticed the popularity of Pepsi and its potential for Latin America, they quickly formed an alliance with it and became one of the largest Pepsi bottlers in the world.[4]

IMITATE AND IMPROVE TO HELP FOCUS YOUR RESOURCES

Practically every one of the billion-dollar entrepreneurs in my interviews kept their focus. When you are competing against other aggressive ventures and corporations managed by smart leaders and you want to dominate your space, you are forced to find a segment to focus on. Targeting the right segment can turn out to be the winning strategy.

Mark Zuckerberg focused on universities to beat better-funded competitors, including MySpace. He first made Facebook the favorite space for Harvard students, and then expanded to Stanford and other universities. He ended up dominating the global linking market.

Sam Walton imitated Target and Kmart when he built big Walmart stores to compete against small retailers. But Sam Walton initially focused on rural America. After dominating this market, he then expanded to the rest of the world.

Medtronic was one of the few companies that did not focus on its hot products in the early years. This nearly caused it to fail. The founders tried to sell it for a few million but there were no takers. So they decided to focus—and became the dominant company in medical electronics.[5]

IMITATE AND IMPROVE TO WIN IN AN EMERGING INDUSTRY

Just as VCs seek ventures with a proven competitive advantage in a high-growth, high-potential, emerging industry, many billion-dollar entrepreneurs also imitate and improve in an emerging industry. By developing an edge in an attractive, emerging industry, these billion-dollar entrepreneurs took off to prove their potential. After proving their potential, some billion-dollar entrepreneurs used VC, and others did not.

Dick Schulze entered the emerging consumer electronics industry by imitating Circuit City in the warehouse-store concept to sell consumer electronics. Schulze improved his competitive advantage with better leadership, and he dominated the industry.

Larry Page and Sergey Brin improved on Internet searches by ranking the results in a logical method (number of incoming links) to show users the most popular sites.

Bill Gates bought an operating system and put Microsoft on the path to dominance by forming an alliance with IBM. With that alliance, he offered a standard to the nascent PC industry and ended up controlling the industry.

Steve Jobs imitated and improved the dominant products with the iPod, iPad, and iPhone and built billion-dollar businesses.

IMITATE AND IMPROVE TO WIN IN A FRAGMENTED INDUSTRY

Fragmented industries have many small companies and no dominant company. Such industries can be highly attractive if entrepreneurs can first get the basics right, and then grow with a trend or develop an advantage to grow.

Bob Kierlin started Fastenal to sell fasteners. He improved his stores by offering better service with trained employees and a better business culture, and then expanded with better-trained managers to dominate the industry.

Steve Ells jumped on the fragmented quick-serve industry and dominated the organic segment as the trend was taking off. Shake Shack has done the same with organic hamburgers.[6]

· · ·

Innovation that relies only on being the first mover is risky. Imitation and improvement to dominate has worked for more. First imitate. Then improve. Then grow and dominate.

CHAPTER 9

Move Fast and Better to Beat Slow and Perfect

It is not necessary to have the "perfect" product. People may be willing to buy a better product or service if it satisfies unmet needs. Don't wait for perfection. Sell and see who buys. Then use their cash to improve.

> "Seeking perfection in product development
> is the enemy of entrepreneurial success."
>
> **—Mark Knudson, founder of five
> successful medical-device ventures**

Timing is key to success. It does not pay to be ahead of customers or behind competitors. It is not necessary to have the perfect product to capture your market. You need the right timing and a better product.

Introduce your product too early, and you may not have a market, or you may spend a lot of money to open up a market for someone else who beats you with a better product or strategy. MySpace was ahead of Facebook, but Facebook won.

Introduce your product too late, and others may already have the momentum to build an insurmountable lead. So you need to get in at the right time, which is like Goldilocks time—not too hot and not too cold.

There are a number of reasons why better beats perfect.

The "Better" Product May Sell

Perhaps the primary reason for introducing a "better" product is that it may sell because it is better than the alternatives available. Often a better product, even if not perfect, can be preferable to existing technologies, and customers will gratefully buy it.

Microsoft's initial operating system may not have been the best operating system possible (from the users' perspective, although Gates benefited), but it was adequate to run the personal computers that customers were buying.

Earl Bakken's initial pacemaker was not battery driven and could not be inserted into the human body. But physicians still used it because it saved lives. The miniature battery and the leads to make an implanted pacemaker came later.

The Cost of "Perfect" May Be Too High

Waiting for the perfect product may not be smart. By delaying, you may allow others to take off and achieve a leadership position that is unassailable. Often, better beats perfect. Some entrepreneurs keep improving their product without trying to sell because they don't know how to sell. Their hope is that customers will beat a path to their door due to the brilliance of their product and ask to buy.

Customers seldom beat a path to any door except perhaps to Steve Jobs's door.

The cost of waiting can be measured in lost time, money, and opportunity. Waiting for perfection may mean that you miss the bus because others grab dominance in the emerging industry and cannot be dislodged by minor improvements to the product.

Mark Twain lost $150,000 investing in a machine that was never introduced for 14 years. The inventor kept hoping for perfection. Others developed and sold better products.[1]

Product Can Be Improved after It Is Introduced—with Cash Flow from Its Own Sales

As noted earlier, Microsoft's operating system and Bakken's pacemaker were improved after the initial product was introduced. But this improvement was paid for by the revenues from the previous not-so-perfect product and not from sophisticated investors who would demand a bigger chunk of the business.

Selling a "Better" Product Can Create Momentum

Companies like Microsoft, Apple, and Medtronic were able to generate momentum and became home runs by getting in as the industry was taking off. This initial momentum attracted attention, free publicity, and money, which helped them grow.

Enter before Relationships Have Solidified

Mature industries have more established relationships between customers and suppliers. Some are solid relationships, which means that there is a strong "brand." Some relationships are tenuous, and a new competitor who is able to add value can take customers away. In general, it is easier to grow by grabbing customers when the industry is young and the relationships have not formed, rather than seeking to break established relationships and increasing market share. Most of the billion-dollar entrepreneurs entered their industries when it was young and emerging and before relationships had solidified.

• • •

To review, here are some suggestions to find the right timing:

- Enter when the industry is young, because established giants in the old technology may not know, or be able to adapt to, the new technology.

- Enter with a better product, service, or business model. Then keep improving to find perfection.

- For proof of viability, check with customers to determine whether they will switch to your better product.

- Enter fast. Then get product superiority. Then develop a more complete platform to satisfy customers' total needs. Then focus on business advantage, such as size and resources, to keep leading the industry, especially when the pace of technology advances slows down.

CHAPTER 10

Improve Backward from the Unmet Need

You can start your business based on what you want to sell—your passion—or based on what customers want to buy—the unmet need. It is important to know your passion, to sell what makes you happy, because you are more likely to spend the long hours to become good at it. But it is also important to know the customers and the unmet need—so you have a market.

"Business is not about what you want to sell.
It's about what people want to buy."

—Dileep Rao

Invention is about technology and the idea. Innovation is about satisfying the unmet needs of customers. Steve Jobs used others' inventions and developed great innovations by improving them to exceed customers' expectations and satisfy their unmet needs. Jobs was not the original creator of great inventions. But he was perhaps the world's greatest imitator and innovator by combining other people's inventions to develop products that people could not resist. (See Figure 7.)

Figure 7. Where do you want to start?

SUPPLY-PUSH MODEL

Too often, researchers and entrepreneurs develop a new product based on their belief that they will find a market. And then they fail. Companies often spend billions on developing new products that customers do not buy. Although some studies dispute the high number, analysts such as Lynn Dornblaser, who studies new products for Mintel, estimates that the percentage of new-product failures can range from 85 to 95 percent.[1] Given the huge amounts corporations spend on marketing and market research, this figure is astounding.

In a supply-push model, entrepreneurs develop a product or service (A in Figure 8) that they think someone needs, and then they seek customers who will buy it (B). Often the technologies are developed before there is a clear market.

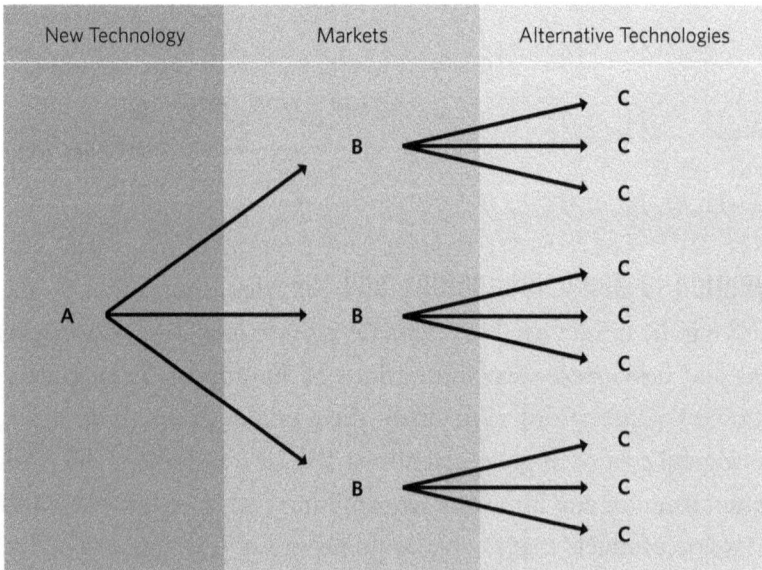

Figure 8. Where do you start?

Supply-push models work well when the technology truly solves a major problem, such as a cure for cancer.

DEMAND-PULL MODEL

In the demand-pull model, entrepreneurs find a market based on customers' unmet needs and then find or develop a better solution to satisfy these needs. This type of opportunity analysis identifies target customers, understands their unmet need, evaluates the value they would derive by satisfying this need, calculates the price they would pay, and estimates the potential size of the market and whether it will be possible to dominate it. If the market is found to be attractive, the product is then developed—or sometimes licensed or acquired. Demand-pull works well when you add sufficient value. When customers are informing you that their current methods are not satisfactory, and you can solve this unmet need, you are more likely to have customers. The greater the value added, the more they are likely to pay.

Demand-based opportunities can also be linked with trends, such as the retirement needs of the baby boomer generation or the potential of the Internet to disrupt large, existing industries. But trend-based ventures can fail if the trend does not materialize as expected, or it does not happen when expected, or it does not grow to the level anticipated. The Internet boom was such a trend. Many entrepreneurs jumped eagerly on board when it first emerged, but it did not grow as fast as expected or expectations ran ahead of reality, causing the dot-com crash of 2000.

Kevin Plank has built Under Armour into a multibillion-dollar company. When Plank was on the University of Maryland football team, he noticed that the cotton T-shirts that the team wore under their uniforms got soaked with their sweat. He concluded that this extra weight diminished their performance, so he came up with a T-shirt made from synthetic fabrics that did not get soaked. He built this idea into a giant company.[2]

When Frederick W. Smith was an undergraduate student at Yale University, he worked as a charter pilot to make money. This is when he noticed that in addition to transporting people, he was also carrying freight for companies that wanted faster delivery than was available from existing options. Using this insight, along with $4 million he inherited from his father and $80 million from venture capitalists, he launched FedEx. While initial demand was slow, and the post office temporarily prevented him from carrying documents, Smith stayed with the venture and built a giant.[3]

Dennis Gillings built Quintiles into one of the largest clinical research organizations in the world. He found the opportunity because a pharmaceutical firm contacted him to solve a problem they were having—some of their test patients were dying and they wanted to find out why. In solving the problem, Gillings realized that the drug giants were better at development than at collecting and analyzing the data. So he founded Quintiles to serve their needs, developed a physician network, checked up on the trials, and hired data-entry experts to make sure the data was accurate. He benefited from a trend of increased outsourcing of new product testing at the big drug companies, and he built Quintiles into a giant with annual revenues of $3 billion.[4]

Knowing customer needs can help you build more profitable and successful ventures than assuming market needs and designing products based on your assumptions.

Why Backward Improvement Is Important

IMPROVE BACKWARD FOR BETTER OPPORTUNITIES
WITH REDUCED PERSONAL BIAS

Knowing your potential (or current) customers and their unmet needs can reduce your personal bias about their needs and enable you to find the best customers.

Dan Cohen (CNS/Breathe Right) is a physician and claims not to know business or sales. *What he did do well, however, was listen to potential customers and see how he could satisfy their unmet needs.* When the barriers were high in one area, he adjusted to find another market that needed his technology. Obviously, it would have helped if, before spending large amounts of money and time, he had checked to see if surgeons were amenable to purchasing equipment that recorded the details of operations, including the errors which would be potentially damaging in a lawsuit. But he did the next-best thing, which was to find another need where he could apply his already-developed solution. This is not the ideal way to do things, but it's perhaps acceptable when you are trying to keep a business alive. Based on the feedback that he received from potential customers, Cohen searched for other opportunities for the already-developed technology, and he found one in sleep-disorder diagnostics. The industry was hobbled by its inability to analyze records fast enough, and CNS filled the void. Within two years, the company was selling more sleep-disorder diagnostics, and the old business died.[5]

Dietrich Mateschitz started Red Bull and built it into a $5 billion-plus company. He discovered the drink when he was visiting Thailand to sell other products. He heard about a beverage that the locals raved about, and as the story goes, when he drank it, his jet lag disappeared. But Mateschitz did not rely on a sample size of one (i.e., himself). When he read that the biggest corporate taxpayer in Japan was someone who sold similar tonics, Mateschitz formed an alliance with the Thai businessman who had developed the drink, carbonated it, and launched his company.[6]

IMPROVE BACKWARD TO OFFER MORE VALUE
THAN YOUR COMPETITORS

If you want to attract customers who will stick with you, the benefits to customers from switching to you should far exceed their cost of switching. This means you need to make them happier than your competitors do, and keep them happier.

Michael Dell (Dell) built his company into a leader in the PC industry by customizing computers to customers' specifications. But the key to his success at adding value was that he was able to buy the latest technology, since he purchased the components after he got the order. His competitors used retail channels, and their PCs were older due to the inefficiency of their supply chains. This allowed Dell to offer higher value to customers and obtain more attractive margins.

IMPROVE BACKWARD FOR HAPPIER CUSTOMERS

Financial leverage (borrowing money) can help you control your assets with limited equity, but it can mean higher risk if you cannot repay the loan. *Customer* leverage can help you obtain more customers by making them happier with fewer resources. This can give you the power of incumbency, which is the reluctance of many customers to switch to other suppliers if they are happy with their current vendors and if the value added by switching is minimal. The power of incumbency is usually a handicap for newer entrepreneurs who seek to dislodge existing vendors, because the benefit of switching has to significantly exceed the cost of switching.

John Mackey built Whole Foods into a retail giant in green products and sustainable living by targeted customization offering higher value to customers. According to Kate Wendt of Wells Fargo, that is their "secret sauce."[7] Stores are allowed to customize to account for regional tastes and specialties, and 20 to 50 percent of the inventory in a store could be different from the others.

As a youth, Richard Copeland (Thor Construction) did the traditional teenage entrepreneurial activities (the basis of many entrepreneurial success stories) of newspaper routes and shoveling sidewalks. As his business grew, he found that he could be the person who brought in the contracts for his odd jobs, kept the customers happy, and collected the money. And he could leverage his time by getting his sisters and neighborhood kids to do the work alongside him. This allowed him to build his outfit beyond a one-man business. Some of his "employees" tried to steal his customers. But Copeland held on to his customers because he had developed a bond with them, with his philosophy to make them happy, and they were eager to see a young entrepreneur grow, especially one who was enthusiastic and willing to offer good service. His customers did not switch.

Jerry Murrell (Five Guys) has built a national giant with sales in excess of $1 billion in the "better burger" category. The company focuses on selling only burgers and fries, adding a few other items just recently. By concentrating on burgers and fries, and constantly seeking to improve them, the company wants to keep its products as a customer favorite. The burgers are fresh (not frozen) and made by hand. The fries, which are also fresh, are made from potatoes grown in colder areas for "denser texture."[8]

IMPROVE BACKWARD TO ATTRACT MORE CUSTOMERS

When you satisfy customers' needs and do it better than others, they come to you and stay with you. Know what they want. This is basic stuff. But knowing it is easy. Doing is hard.

Sam Walton wanted to be more competitive on pricing than the existing small retailers of rural America. So he focused on a clean store, but he did not invest much to make it attractive.

Steve Jobs knew he was selling innovative products that were beautiful. As he put it, "we stand at the intersection of art and science." He even designed a staircase that he patented and had it installed in Apple's stores. And he took his staff to a museum exhibition of Tiffany glass to see beautiful designs. He knew his customers and what they wanted.[9]

Jeff Bezos (Amazon.com) is a cross between Walton and Jobs. Like Jobs, he is part of the Internet age. Like Walton, he knows that his customers want competitive prices. With his low-cost approach, Bezos can afford to offer low prices and drive margins down and destroy competitors. According to Bezos, "Your margin is my opportunity."[10]

IMPROVE BACKWARD TO REDUCE THE TIME TO
REACH PROFITABLE SALES

By getting customers faster, you can get revenues and reach profitability sooner, assuming, of course, that you can control your overhead and keep it low. So it helps to know your customers and their unmet needs.

Norman Nie started SPSS while finishing his doctoral dissertation at Stanford University. He had massive amounts of numbers to crunch and analyze, and he realized he could not do it all manually. So, together with two partners, he started working on a program that could analyze the data for his research needs. Knowing that other professors and researchers also had massive amounts of numbers to crunch, Nie and his partners started offering the program to them at $400 per tape, which was the amount they could spend without departmental authorization (so know your customers and their spending limits). Without any venture capital, they built their company and sold it to IBM in 2009 for $1.2 billion.[11]

• • •

In summation, billion-dollar entrepreneurs are good at working backward from customers' unmet needs. They excel at understanding these needs and making customers happier with advanced technologies, not at inventing the technology.

CHAPTER 11

Seek a Platform for Long-Term Potential

There are two types of platforms. The first is a product platform, which combines advances on multiple fronts to develop a product that offers a higher level of benefits with a technology advantage. The other is a market platform, which combines products and services from multiple vendors in the same outlet to offer the complete set of benefits and convenience that customers seek. Both types of platforms can offer more long-term, competitive advantages than relying only on your own technology advances or on your own products.

> "Products may offer limited benefits to a few. Platforms satisfy multiple needs for many."
>
> **—Dileep Rao**

Based on their degree of innovation, which is the level of change from existing offerings, new products can range from revolutionary (breakthrough) to evolutionary (derivatives), the latter featuring improvements to existing products.[1]

Revolutionary (breakthrough) products are major departures from existing products, whether in the nature of the product itself, or in the process involved, or the materials used. As an example, personal computers were a revolutionary change from mainframe computers, and the Internet was a radical departure from historical ways of retailing, investing, connecting, and getting information. Revolutionary products are usually based on technology breakthroughs and are quite different from existing products. At the start, customers often find it difficult to evaluate these revolutionary advances or understand why they should use them or buy them, because they are so radically different from existing products. And often at the start, these revolutionary advances may not offer the degree of benefits that the vast majority of established customers seek.

Evolutionary (or derivative) products are "minor" advances or improvements on existing products, and they are funded and introduced by companies mainly to keep their products updated and competitive. Usually products are improved along one dimension, such as making an existing product better or cheaper, or incorporating new technologies, designs, and colors. This type of product improvement is usually based more on market research and feedback from customers who often help improve existing products based on their likes and dislikes.

In the middle are platforms. Platform advances fall between revolutionary and evolutionary development, and can be characterized as follows:

- *New product (or service) platforms* combine various technologies, some of which are new and others that are existing. These product platforms can have many dimensions of change, such as changes in cost, quality, or performance, and can offer dramatically new and unique benefits. Examples of such platform products include the Sony Walkman, which developed a new technology, or the Apple iTunes that legally combined multiple technologies and products to create a blockbuster platform. These product platforms are less risky and cheaper to develop than revolutionary products but with more potential and differentiation than evolutionary advances. Steve Jobs was the master at this, having developed platform products like the iPod, the iPad, and the iPhone.

- *New retail platforms* allow products or services to be sold in a new way. One example is the big-box concept, such as Walmart's big stores in small towns. Or it can be a new type of technology platform that can be used to sell other products, such as the Amazon.com platform that allowed the company to sell many types of products and services to a wide variety of customers in a new way.

Product platforms can be less expensive to develop than revolutionary products, but they have more potential and differentiation than evolutionary advances. Platforms also give you an advantage over indirect competitors by making it difficult for existing businesses to copy you easily. And you can replace obsolete products and services in your retail platform with newer ones to stay competitive.

Why Platforms Are Desirable

Many entrepreneurial successes are built on platforms. A platform allows the business to grow in multiple markets against multiple competitors. It allows the company to adjust to changing times, technologies, and trends. A platform offers a company a way to change the rules of the game and to develop a competitive edge. Perhaps most important, it allows entrepreneurs to build a stronger competitive position against incumbent companies than just using evolutionary advances.

PLATFORMS ALLOW FOLLOW-ON PRODUCTS AND SERVICES FOR GROWTH WITH REDUCED RISK AND COST

Platforms allow entrepreneurs to make a more dramatic change from the status quo, develop a competitive position, and build a channel that can be used to sell more related products and services. A platform creates more of an impact than a single product and lays the foundation for growth with follow-on products and services.

When Ron Shaich was building his first chain, Au Bon Pain, he found that French baked products were becoming a commodity. He had to make changes to continue growing. So he grew with soups, salads, and sandwiches, with croissants and bread as platforms.[2]

PLATFORMS ARE MORE CAPITAL-EFFICIENT THAN REVOLUTIONARY

Introducing a platform can also be more capital-efficient. Platform products based on existing technologies do not have the high research and development costs of revolutionary products. They are also more difficult to copy than small, evolutionary innovations. Combining newly introduced revolutionary technologies with existing products, but doing it in new ways, can offer immense benefits. Any testing needed is done in the application aspect of the platform and the business model, not in the product development phase.

Sam Walton used his big-box platform store in small towns. He avoided the other big-box stores, since they were competing in urban areas, and Walton got a free pass in his rural market.

Jeff Bezos has used his platform to expand into many types of products and services.

PLATFORMS HELP YOU BUILD A COMPETITIVE ECOSYSTEM

A complete ecosystem allows you to build a new business model that is often difficult for competitors to catch. By offering a complete line of products and services that customers seek, and with convenience and competitive prices, a complete ecosystem can make customers happier and keep them tied to your business.

Perhaps the master of this strategy was Steve Jobs. His platforms included entire companies. At Pixar, he changed the old system of movie production by keeping the same team of creative and business types who developed endless hits. The company was the platform. At Apple, after his return, he built platforms for music (iPod), cell phones (iPhone), and computers (iPad). Apple's operating system can also be considered a platform, since it can be used across Apple's computers and phones.[3]

Michael Dell made his business model of selling PCs directly to consumers into a platform to sell a variety of PC-related products through the same supply chain.

Jeff Bezos made Amazon.com a platform for everything under the sun.

• • •

Before focusing only on a product, consider the total needs and experience of the ultimate customer. To make your platform more competitive, examine your customers' unmet needs and your competitors' weaknesses. Then seek the right technology advances and jump on the right, emerging trends.

CHAPTER 12

Improve Frequently for Happier Customers

To succeed, you need to make your customers happier than your competitors can. And you need to do this without a lot of capital, if you are like most entrepreneurs. Rather than seeking to do this with one big development, most billion-dollar entrepreneurs focused on many small improvements that did not cost much but made customers happier, especially when their impacts were combined.

"I'll either buy you a house or I'll dress you in mourning."
—El Cordobés, the matador, speaking to his sister

Gamblers go for the big score. El Cordobés's statement is a gamble and a commitment. Luckily for him (and his sister), he became one of the most successful matadors in Spanish history.

You have to be better than your competitors by a high enough level to get customers to switch to you. To do this, billion-dollar entrepreneurs seek many small improvements rather than seeking the one magic elixir. The odds are that the blockbuster improvement may be tough to develop, or take too long, or cost too much, or not do enough, or be easily imitated. By using many small improvements, you are more likely to get an edge.

VCs can afford to take giant risks. John Doerr lost $100 million in Segway.[1] Most entrepreneurs need to develop their business with less risk.

Customers Don't Change Easily from Established Patterns

Customers don't switch vendors or change buying patterns casually. Usually, they don't switch for "as good as," and if they switch for a few pennies (because you have decided to enter the market as a lower-priced entry), they may also leave for a few pennies offered by your larger competitors to keep them. Potential customers consider the benefits, and the costs and risks, of the switch. If the benefits far out-weigh the costs and the risks, and they are aware of your company, and the risk is not very high, they may switch.

David Duffield started PeopleSoft in 1987 and sold it to Oracle in 2004 for $10.3 billion.[2] He started his second company, Workday, after a three-month retirement. Workday, which has Michael Dell and Jeff Bezos as its investors, expects to reach bookings in excess of $500 million, while competing in a fierce market against Oracle and SAP. To do this, Workday is focusing on customer happiness at lower cost by using many strategies. One is the use of cloud computing to reduce costs, and because it allows more frequent improvements than enterprise software does. It is also cheaper because customers can add capacity as they need it. Most important, Workday's CEO, Aneel Bhusri, who was with Duffield at PeopleSoft, gave top priority to making the customer experience friendly and easy to use, and "as simple to learn as shopping on Amazon.com."[3]

Sticky Customers Stay, Buy More, and Pay More

What is the first priority of a business? Financial experts maintain that it is a return on investment. But this is a question of what comes first, the chicken or the egg? Is there a way to get a good return on investment—for the long term—by not having loyal, sticky, and happier customers? These are customers who keep coming back, who buy more, and who pay more.

Steve Jobs built the Apple "franchise" into the most valuable company in the world by getting rabid fans, not just happier customers. By paying attention to every detail of the product and service, and by transforming Apple into a mark of elegance, he was able to set prices that could only make others drool. Interestingly, he did it not by coming up with new products and services, but by making existing ones better than the first movers (as in iPod, iPad, and iPhone).

But keeping customers after you attract them can also be expensive if you must rely on cutting prices to keep them, or if your competitors can add more convenience for the same price. Price-sensitive customers may switch to the lowest-price vendor, and that may not be you. By making customers happier than your competitors can, you can keep them and be able to charge them more. By keeping them, you can reduce your lifetime marketing cost per customer. Being able to charge more means that you increase your profits per customer. And happier customers tell others, which can also reduce your cost of marketing.

The Internet browser wars between Netscape and Explorer offered a dramatic example of the value of offering more convenience. Netscape started out with about a 90 percent market share, but when the better-heeled and stronger Microsoft put Netscape in the bull's-eye and combined Explorer with its other software, customers switched to Explorer. Netscape did not make customers happy enough.

Sticky customers help you to dominate the segment. When you are better, customers return, are loyal, and pay more. This can avoid price wars with competitors who may have more resources and can cut prices more easily. By making customers happier and avoiding price wars, you not only get repeat business but also avoid debilitating competition.

Horst Rechelbacher (Aveda) was in an auto accident in the Midwest on one of his trips to the United States from Austria. To pay his hospital bills, he got a job in a salon in downtown Minneapolis. He became instantly successful with his attention to customer happiness. His customers kept coming back, and Rechelbacher had all the clients he needed and more. The other hair designers in the salon wanted to work with him to profit from his happier customers. After three months, in a salon of nine hairdressers, he had two assistants and was earning more money than the others. He had an average of 35 clients per day while the others had six to seven.[4]

Happier Customers Refer Others

When you are better, customers tell others. Word of mouth (also called viral marketing by the mavens who develop hip buzzwords for previously simple concepts) is a great marketing tool, but it only seems to work for exceptional people, products, and services. Referrals from customers are perhaps the best source of new customers, since no financial outlay is needed to promote and advertise the product beyond what's needed to make customers happier. It is difficult to forecast whether any product will go viral, but your odds seem better if you make customers happier.

Intuit was conceived by Scott Cook and founded by Cook and Tom Proulx in 1983. Today it is a company with revenues exceeding

$5 billion and a market cap exceeding $44 billion (February 27, 2018). When Intuit first introduced Quicken, its flagship tax software, there were many others also on the market. Financially, Intuit did not do well. All of this changed when Intuit started to market its products directly to customers and made them happier by customizing the software for each segment. The initial customers were very happy with the product, and they in turn mentioned this to others, causing Intuit to dominate this space. Happier customers refer others.[5]

Horst Rechelbacher's initial clients were well-to-do Jewish women in Minneapolis. The Jewish community in Minneapolis was a close-knit group, and they talked to each other. One of his clients was a banker. She knew of another hair salon that had failed, and its equipment was available for a reasonable price. She was also willing to lend Rechelbacher $4,000 to buy the equipment and start his salon. All the other hairdressers at the initial salon wanted to come with him, since he was teaching them how to style hair. With the $4,000 loan, Rechelbacher started his salon. Within three months, his was the busiest salon in Minneapolis.[6]

Why Make Frequent Improvements?

Seeking a giant blockbuster technology, such as a cure for cancer, usually costs more money than most entrepreneurs have. And most VCs are reluctant to offer funding for research. So entrepreneurs are forced to rely on themselves and their ability to build customer loyalty without capital. This often means making many small improvements, doing it more frequently, doing it with the cash flow from the previous improvements, and offering superior service to keep customers happier.

YOU DON'T HAVE THE FUNDS TO DEVELOP
MAJOR TECHNOLOGIES

Bob Kierlin built Fastenal into the largest fastener company in the United States by offering better service than anyone else. Each employee was encouraged to work with other employees to offer customers what they wanted and when they wanted it. He recruited his sales force straight out of college before they could accumulate bad habits elsewhere. And he recruited those with empathy—the ones who do not leave their carts in the middle of the aisle in a grocery store.

One Friday, the Ford Motor Company wanted a part for an expensive machine over a weekend. The alternative was to get the part from the vendor with a lengthy delay. Fastenal worked overtime during the weekend, hired a pilot to deliver the part on Sunday night, and made sure the equipment was working on Monday morning, saving Ford hundreds of thousands of dollars. Fastenal got a loyal customer.[7]

• • •

Maybe it is a cliché, but the entrepreneur's work is never done. There is always someone nipping at your heels and other parts of your anatomy. Keep improving for happier customers.

PART III

STRATEGY FOR MORE EDGE PER DOLLAR

> When your product (or service) can be easily imitated, your advantage needs to be in other aspects of your business. One of the most important of these other aspects is your business strategy. The right strategy can get you an edge. The best strategy can get you an edge—without venture capital.

Products are what you sell. Strategy is how you win.

There are complicated definitions of business strategies, which include products sold, customers targeted, value added, competitive differentiation, marketing strategy, and financial performance. But at the basic level, a business strategy includes the "three legs of the stool" for any business opportunity—

- What you sell: your product or service

- Whom will you sell to: your target customer segment

- Who will keep you from selling: your competitors

These three key factors influence the value you add, your customers' happiness, pricing, marketing strategy, financial needs, and financial performance. You need to focus on these three factors first.

The right business strategy can influence your advantage, your needs, and your level of success. Steve Jobs, Bill Gates, and Michael Dell can safely be added to any list of great entrepreneurs, and they are a good study of differing business strategies in the same emerging industry, which was PCs. They did not spend fortunes on developing their technology. All of them started in their late teens or early 20s. But that is where the similarities end. Table 5 shows key similarities and differences.

TABLE 5. STRATEGIES USED BY JOBS, GATES, AND DELL

	APPLE	MICROSOFT	DELL
Industry stage	Emerging	Emerging	Emerging
Unique advantage	Internally developed OS	Licensed OS	Business model
Strategy	VC-traditional	VC-delayer	VC-avoider
Wealth kept/ Wealth created	0.7%	31%	50%

Jobs had a capital-intensive strategy. He entered the industry as it was emerging. He developed his product with Steve Wozniak and sold his PCs to consumers and businesses while competing against many other newly formed PC companies. He sought to differentiate his product with his own internal technology and operating system when the world was adopting the Wintel standard. His strategy was capital-dependent, with high needs for marketing and promotion, overhead, and assets (inventory, receivables, etc.). Because of his high capital needs, he had to get VC early, which caused him to lose control of the company. When the Macintosh did not live up to initial expectations, the VCs fired him.

Gates used a hybrid, delayed-VC strategy. Gates, along with Paul Allen, started Microsoft to write software for the emerging PC industry. Their strategy was not capital-intensive and was funded with personal capital and cash flow. When Gates found that IBM was seeking an operating system for its planned line of PCs, he bought one and licensed it to IBM on a non-exclusive basis. The IBM alliance made Microsoft's operating system the industry standard and established Microsoft at the center of the PC universe. By delaying the investment from VCs (and he is said to have obtained VC just to get someone with gray hair as an investor and on his board), Gates could pick the VC he wanted, keep control of Microsoft, and stay on as CEO.[1]

Dell used a capital-efficient, VC-avoidance strategy. Dell started selling customized PCs directly to customers. By making PCs to order, he could differentiate his products and business from others who were selling standardized PCs via retail channels—for attractive margins. Since he was buying the parts and assembling the PC after the order, he could use the latest technology. Most important, his customers paid him cash when they ordered, and Dell was able to use this cash as working capital. This business model allowed him to use the latest components that were often more efficient at lower prices, charge the same as competitors who made PCs earlier with older components to fill the retail pipeline, avoid the discount offered to retailers because he sold direct to customers, and grow without VC. When asked why he developed his model to sell customized PCs without inventory, Dell noted that he had no money to buy inventory. This supposed disadvantage and resulting strategy made him his fortune.

By delaying VC, Gates kept 31 percent of the wealth created in Microsoft.[2] Dell kept 50 percent of the wealth created in his company. At the time of his death, Jobs "only" had about 0.7 percent of Apple's worth, which was still in the billions. That was his reward for leading one of the greatest turnarounds in business history. He had this level of wealth from Apple due to stock options he got when he returned to Apple.

As noted before, most high-performance, billion-dollar entrepreneurs either avoided VC if they were outside Silicon Valley, or delayed VC if they were in Silicon Valley. By doing so, these entrepreneurs had the freedom to develop the opportunity for high potential and to find the strategy that helped them grow with dominance without interference from the outside.

Billion-dollar entrepreneurs grew without capital or with delayed VC by following these seven rules:

1. Win with Goldilocks goals.

2. Differentiate for your entry wedge.

3. Grow with the segment from heaven.

4. Target the right strategic group to dominate and grow.

5. Develop value in your strategy.

6. Price for value, growth, and cash flow.

7. Prove your strategy and its value.

CHAPTER 13

Strategy VC-Style

VCs want proof of potential, especially if the strategy is also developed and proven. Strategy is particularly important when the technology does not have strong patent protection and is not a billion-dollar technology (as is the case for most technologies). Entrepreneurs have to bring their product (or service) to the stage where there is proof of potential, and this means proving that the strategy can build a giant company.

> "VCs invest little in great ideas because there are few great ideas. They prefer ventures with proven strategies to dominate high-potential, emerging industries."
>
> **—Dileep Rao**

VCs have financed companies like Intel, Google, eBay, and Netflix. They have mainly done well when they can invest a lot of money and earn a very high return. The requirement to invest a lot of money and earn high returns influences their business model.

VCs Have Big Goals

VCs want home runs. Entrepreneurs should not seek VC if their goal is to not to build a huge business and do it rapidly. Businesses that create the most value (wealth) in a relatively short time period are the most highly sought after by VCs and by sophisticated investors. If your business cannot dominate an emerging high-growth industry, your chances of getting VC, at least from the Silicon Valley firms, are very small. To raise large amounts of financing from sophisticated investors, entrepreneurs need to have a goal and a plan to build value in direct proportion to the amount of investment needed in the shortest time period possible and to provide an attractive exit for investors. The odds of achieving all these goals are slim.

During the height of the dot-com boom, some VCs were even suggesting at VC forums that entrepreneurs should not bother them with companies that had less than a billion-dollar potential. Some of them invested in failures like Webvan, Pets.com, and Segway.

But having high goals is not enough. You also need to achieve them. If you cannot perform to your plan, the VCs might replace you as the leader or sell the business to recoup their investment.

VCs Seek Emerging High-Potential Industries and Markets

In general, VCs prefer ventures with a long-term competitive advantage to capture a huge market share with high margins in emerging industries that have huge potential. Often, the result is that many VC-funded ventures pile into the same "hot" industries.

VCs also seek ventures that have the momentum to dominate these emerging industries. They invest heavily in these ventures to seek dominance and erect barriers to prevent others from entering.

eBay became dominant in online auctions and grew into the giant it is today. It used VC financing to attract more customers—who in turn lured more vendors—and helped eBay to dominate its industry.

VCs like emerging industries because that is where they can build the next generation of billion-dollar ventures and earn high returns.

As Table 1 showed, VC home runs have mainly been in emerging, high-potential industries.

VCs seek companies in emerging industries that have developed products or services that offer an advantage, as in the case of Google's search engine, or they invest after the momentum has been achieved, as in the case of Facebook and Groupon. Their investments often compete with other VC-funded ventures in the same industry. The venture that dominates the segment wins, and the others often fail.

VCs Do Well When Their Ventures Dominate

The key to success, for VCs and billion-dollar entrepreneurs, was to dominate their industry. Silicon Valley VCs have done well, compared with VCs in the rest of the country, because most of the ventures that have dominated high-potential, emerging industries have been in Silicon Valley.[1] In contrast, high-performance entrepreneurs in Minnesota succeeded in a wide variety of situations, with some developing ventures in emerging industries (39 percent), in niches of established industries (36 percent), or in fragmented industries (21 percent).[2]

VCs Wait until Aha to Reduce Risks

VCs normally invest after the venture's momentum, growth, and differentiation are already established, that is, after Aha. To this exciting combination, they add money and resources to build a giant corporation quickly. They add lots of money to grow fast, raise barriers for others, and become dominant. When it does work, it creates a home run. The best VC investments have been those in which significant levels of money are used to dominate after the momentum has been established.

Both Facebook and eBay got VC after they had established their momentum. But Zuckerberg had established his leadership credentials and stayed on to lead Facebook. Pierre Omidyar was replaced because eBay had not reached the stage where his leadership was proven.

VCs Want Ventures That Sell Smart

The type of customer, and the sales and marketing strategy, can have a major impact on a venture's risk and success. Ventures that serve national consumer markets require complex sales, marketing, and distribution channels, which can be difficult for new ventures without sophisticated management and ample financial resources.

VCs have shown a preference for ventures that sell directly to users and customers. In the pre-Internet era, most VC-funded ventures sold directly to businesses (B2B) due to the relative ease of identifying and targeting potential customers. The Internet changed this by allowing direct sales to national and global consumers. VC-funded ventures in the Internet age include very successful ones that sell online to national and global consumers.

VCs Seek High-Value, High-Margin Products and Services

High-value, high-margin products and services offer additional cash to pay for the increased overhead needed by capital-dependent, high-growth models. Higher margins also help when the venture goes public, because investment bankers and the investing public often have higher valuations for higher-margin businesses (all other things being the same).

In the Internet era, VCs have also practiced the "high-free" strategy, where the consumer version of the product is offered free to the mass market to make the product the standard, and a developer's version with high margins is sold to businesses. Companies are also offered an advertising-based strategy to sell to the consumer market.

Google is a prime example of this strategy. Google offers free searches to the public and makes its profits from paid advertising on its website. Adobe offers tools to consumers at no charge to read the output from its tools that are paid for by users and designers. LinkedIn offers a variation on this concept, where consumers use the basic option for free but are encouraged to use higher-level services for fees.

VCs Invest Huge Amounts for Dominance, but They Do It in Stages

Unlike most angels, VCs invest huge amounts of money. The largest VC funds raise hundreds of millions to invest, and they need to invest this in large chunks to make optimum use of their time. But ventures need smaller amounts in early stages and larger amounts in later stages. This has resulted in high-growth, capital-intensive ventures raising money in stages. In the early stages, they raise small amounts from angels, followed by larger amounts from small, early-stage VC. At later stages, ventures approach the largest VC funds. VC funds also specialize by stage, and later stages of a venture are often funded by different VCs. This means that early-stage ventures specialize in the high-risk stages when the venture is just emerging. The amounts they invest are huge compared with angels but smaller than the amounts provided by later-stage ventures. Due to their higher risk in early stages, these funds also have to earn more from their fewer winners than later-stage funds.

As the venture starts to take off, VCs invest larger amounts to fund the growing needs of the venture, such as costs for sales, marketing, assets, expenses, and so forth. This means that high-growth, capital-intensive ventures need to constantly seek additional funding and, ideally, each new round is at a higher valuation.

VCs hope to exit from the venture at valuations that give them a high, stage-based return either through an IPO or through a strategic sale to a large corporation. Stage-based investing helps the VCs evaluate venture progress and reduce risk.

While VCs invested a higher proportion in early stages in the go-go years of the Internet boom in the late 1990s, since 2001, VCs have invested a very small percent of their total investments in the seed stage (see Table 6). The VCs' strategy of waiting until they see business momentum and proof of the business model before they invest large amounts can increase the entrepreneur's risk. If VCs do not invest in the later stages, the venture may fold.

TABLE 6. PERCENT OF VC INVESTMENTS IN SEED/EARLY STAGES

YEAR	SEED STAGE (% OF TOTAL)	SEED + EARLY STAGE (% OF TOTAL)
2002	0.26	15.7
2003	0.24	12.6
2004	0.75	14.2
2005	0.38	17.8
2006	0.83	16.8
2007	0.73	19.0
2008	0.71	19.2
2009	1.67	19.5
2010	1.99	17.1
2011	2.26	19.2
2012	3.6	21.9
2013	4.3	23.5
2014	3.58	18.3
2015	2.97	18.6
2016	3.78	21.5
2017	3.17	18.5

PriceWaterhouse Coopers/NVCA MoneyTree™ Report

When VCs invest early, before the venture, it may have more to do with the potential of a technology to build a billion-dollar company. Genentech got VC funding by developing the technology to splice the gene. But if the initial business model does not work, VCs may sell the intellectual property to recoup their investment, or fire the entrepreneur and find another CEO to run the business, which can significantly dilute the entrepreneur's stake.

• • •

Consider VC if you are in Silicon Valley. About 90 percent of Silicon Valley's billion-dollar entrepreneurs used VC, compared with 9 percent outside. Silicon Valley VCs have found the secret to building giant companies in emerging industries. Outside Silicon Valley, entrepreneurs may be better off without VC. But even in Silicon Valley, 75 percent delayed VC until they had proven their technology potential, business potential, and leadership potential.

CHAPTER 14

Win with Goldilocks Goals

What are the right goals for you? Your goals can influence your plan and your projections. Should you shoot for the moon and seek dominance even when there is no evidence that you can get it, and fund and spend accordingly? Or should you have prudent goals and raise your sights as your business grows?

"Seek goals at the upper end of talent and the lower end of hopes."

—Dileep Rao

Are you developing your projections for real reasons or spurious ones? Real projections are within the range of what you think is possible based on a realistic analysis of your market, competitors, industry growth, financial and managerial resources, and competitive advantage. Spurious projections are done to influence investors, to try to convince them that you have a hot venture, and to seek a high valuation for your business. My experience has been that projections are always presented to investors as "conservative projections." They seldom are. Very few entrepreneurs have developed projections based on real proof where the odds of success are reasonable. Most entrepreneurs are simply guessing and hoping that someone believes their guesses.

Can you accurately predict the future to set realistic goals? If you can predict with any level of accuracy for a startup, you belong in the forecaster's hall of fame. You will be the first inductee. John Kenneth Galbraith once said that there are two kinds of forecasters, "those who know they don't know and those who don't know they don't know."

Projections seldom come true in new ventures (I say that with 99.9 percent confidence). By being aware, you will use projections for the true reason entrepreneurs should do projections—to know if you are heading in the right direction after you start, or are heading off the cliff.

You should seek realistic and challenging goals, which are at the upper end of your talent and the lower end of hopes. To be credible, the venture's goals should be consistent with the scale of the opportunity and the track record of management. A venture that depends on achieving an overly optimistic (based on history and the industry) growth rate or capturing an unrealistic market share (based on history and advantage) may not be credible.

Along with business goals, it also helps to know your personal goals. In other words, what do *you* want from the venture, and what are you willing to give up to achieve this goal? If you want to stay in control of the business, you may need to develop a plan that does not rely on getting venture capital at an early stage. In Silicon Valley and in emerging industries, it is viable to get VC after Aha—but you need to take it to Aha. Outside Silicon Valley and in more mature industries, it pays to seek a capital-efficient plan because there are very few VCs, and even fewer successful VCs.

Knowing what you want your business to be is quite useful because each goal may require a different strategy and have different levels of credibility. Goals can include, among others, the level and timing of sales, net income, market share, valuation, or return on investment that you want to achieve. Your goals should reflect your opportunity and skills, and influence your plan and strategies. Goals can also show your long-term direction, including whether you want to have an initial public offering, assuming, of course, that you have the opportunity to go public.

Goals influence financing. Ventures with the goal and potential to dominate high-growth, emerging markets may attract angel capital and VC. The question for you is whether you want it and need it and when. Contrarily, if your goal is to retain control of your venture, angel or venture capital may not be right for you.

Your goals can also deal with your market and industry. You may want to grow faster than your industry and achieve market leadership, or grow with the industry, or achieve a defined level of profit and cash flow, which could mean more focused sales. Each goal has impacts. The goal of high growth in a slow-growth industry may require acquisitions or a price war where few may win. Each goal influences your financing. High growth may need VC, and acquisitions may need access to capital or debt.

Achievable and credible goals are preferred by billion-dollar entrepreneurs for several reasons.

Credibility Is Like Money in the Bank

Whether you are seeking financing from equity sources, lenders, vendors, customers, or from internal cash, realistic goals and achievable projections enhance credibility. Miss your projections and financiers are unlikely to take you seriously. Achieving projections helps enhance credibility and helps you get the right financing from the right sources at the right time with the right terms.

Sophisticated investors, including venture capitalists, like to invest in businesses with high potential. But if investors perceive venture goals to be unrealistic visions and wishful thinking, and you have missed them in the past, they may not take you seriously. They will assume that you are inflating projections to achieve unrealistic valuations. Or they fire you if you do not achieve your projections, in which case, you will lose control of the business.

But if you are too conservative in your projections, VCs may not invest, since they may not see you as having high potential. Investors like to invest in high-growth companies for high-level returns. Lenders like to see you make realistic projections that you achieve, especially for cash flow, since they get repaid from your cash flow. Their alternative is to foreclose on the loan, which is not pleasant. Vendors sometimes offer extended terms, but they want you to control cash flow and pay when due. With all financiers and creditors, credibility is key. It is like having money in the bank.

Seeking High Valuation in Minimum Time Means That You Are Going for Broke

VCs want to maximize the venture's valuation because they are seeking high returns from their home runs to pay for the losing ventures in their portfolio and to give an attractive return to their investors. However, a key problem with the VC model is that about 80 percent of VC-funded ventures fail to reach expectations, so your odds are not good. Even in the 20 percent of ventures that do reach expectations, you, the entrepreneur, may not do well. Get VC early and you may have to give control to the VCs who recruit a professional CEO. You suffer dilution at the hands of both. It might be better to have goals to achieve momentum before seeking VC, and wait for the VCs to agree to your terms. That's what entrepreneurs like Gates and Zuckerberg did.

Traditional Models Emphasize Growth with Cash Flow

Corporations rely on internal cash flow to pay for growth and dividends. The corporate model usually seeks to "optimize" the level of sales, profits (earnings per share), and cash flow. This means that they mostly seek cash-flow-based growth, and their growth may be slower because they mainly operate in mature industries. High-performance entrepreneurs want to grow fast but with control. So they need to balance growth needs with cash flow and external financing.

• • •

Capital-intensive, VC-seeking entrepreneurs have aggressive growth rates because VCs want high growth rates and high potential valuation. Billion-dollar entrepreneurs try to have tempered goals. They need to do a balancing act to be high enough to be a leader in the industry and low enough to be able to grow with control and cash flow. After Aha, they accelerate their growth rate to dominate their industry. This acceleration was funded from sources controlled by the entrepreneur.

CHAPTER 15

Differentiate for Your Entry Wedge

Why should your customers switch from their existing vendors to you? Many entrepreneurs seek to enter the marketplace by reducing prices. Is this wise?

> "If you can't differentiate, you can't differentially price. If you can't differentially price, you have no market power, and you can't create any profits."
> **—Scott McNealy, former CEO, Sun Microsystems**

Many entrepreneurs seek to find their differentiation before they launch their businesses. But what looks good on paper may not work in practice. The final proof of differentiation is in the marketplace, not on the plan.

To grow and create profits, you need to differentiate based on market needs and your competitive strengths. The entry wedge can take many forms and can include new technologies (Medtronic), new business models (Dell), new locations (Walmart), or better leadership (Jobs, Bezos).

The first step is to know where your venture can get an edge over your competitors and then develop marketing, operations, management, and resource strategies that are consistent with that edge. To develop your competitive advantage, the key is not only about what you want to sell and how you want to sell it. It helps to start with *what the customer wants to buy and their unmet need.*

Understand the difference between features and benefits to develop your differentiation. Marketing guru Theodore Levitt said, "People don't want to buy a quarter-inch drill, they want to buy a quarter-inch hole!" Charles Revson of Revlon Cosmetics noted, "In the factory, we make cosmetics; in the store, we sell hope." This is an excellent analysis of the difference between the company's understanding of what it is selling and the customers' perception of what they are buying. With six words, Revson defined the importance of the difference between the features of the product and its benefits. To be a high-performance entrepreneur, you need to understand not just the features of the product but, more important, its benefits.

Features define what you are selling. Benefits define what customers are buying. You can define your product in terms of its features, such as size, speed, design, weight, price, or selection. You may have the smallest product, the one with the most bells and whistles, or the fastest. But the key question is whether customers value these features and will pay more for these features. And you need to consider how long you can maintain your advantage before competitors erase it.

Benefits should be considered from the perspective of the customers: Why are they buying? Understanding the benefits helps you understand how the product satisfies customers' unmet needs. If lipstick was sold like a chemical, the beauty companies would be selling it in industrial-size drums at a price of cents per pound. By selling lipsticks as "glamour" to make women look beautiful, and using gorgeous models, cosmetics manufacturers sell small quantities at high prices with great margins.

The Right Wedge Gives Customers a Reason to Switch

When you start a new business or seek new customers, you want to make your potential customers switch from their current source of satisfaction—your competitor—to you. Your competitor can be a direct competitor who satisfies the same customer's similar needs and sells the same product in the same way, or an indirect competitor who has a different business model but satisfies the same need, or you may not have a competitor, which means that the need may not exist, and you have to create the need. This means that you need an entry wedge that gives you some advantage so you don't get into a price war—especially when you have fewer resources and customers than your competitors. The key question is why would anyone switch from what they are now using to you? If they switch because of your lower price, are you starting a price war, and do you have more resources and abilities than established companies to survive a price war? With lower prices, will you have the profit margins and cash flow, and can you stay in business and succeed? Your goal is not just to get sales but to make profits (or get a positive cash flow).

Find the entry wedge where value exceeds price. Every market segment has its own buying influencers—the benefits and rewards of buying compared with the costs and risks. These are the hot buttons that influence buying and the barriers that may keep buyers away, assuming they know enough about your product. To find the right entry wedge, you need to know your customers' motivations and why they will buy from you. Different customers may have varied motivations. For some, price is key. For others, it could be prestige. For others still, it could be convenience. Find the real reasons customers buy your type of products to satisfy their true needs, which can help you obtain a higher market share and higher profitability.

Don Kotula started Northern Tool to sell log splitters. As a teenager, Kotula helped his dad sell various kinds of equipment and trucks. Based on customer requests, Kotula started his own business to sell hydraulics equipment to his dad's customers. His customers also told him that they were looking for a log splitter that could be used by farmers and loggers. After getting his degree and working for a major airline, Kotula decided to get back to his own business, and he started with log splitters. He wrote a booklet on how to build a log splitter and sold this booklet for a nominal cost to find those who were genuinely interested in buying a log splitter. Then he sold parts for the log splitter, and the customers made their own frame. Later he had a supplier make the frame. Kotula had found the perfect entry point for the "he-man" do-it-yourself market.

It is important to know the *real reasons* why the customer is buying, or will buy, the product and not just why *you* think they are buying or not buying. Often the benefits are not obvious. Many early technology adapters buy to make a statement about themselves as avant-garde or cool and not necessarily because the price is low. Knowing the precise benefits helps you to spot trends before competitors; to price based on the benefits; to influence product development, packaging, and advertising; to target the best market segments; and to view the business from the perspective of the user.

Lloyd Sigel built Lloyd's Barbeque by communicating the benefits of his product. He was selling beef that had already been barbecued. So he built a fake barbecue pit and had his packaged product rotating on it to show that it had already been cooked. The product sold. Sigel was able to demonstrate and sell the right benefits: precooked food to save time for women who had started working outside the home and did not have much time to cook dinner.

Knowing the Value Proposition Helps Sales and Margins

The value that customers get by buying from you is your value proposition. An entry wedge with a sustainable advantage to offer high value helps you obtain higher profit margins. The higher the value, the greater the price customers are likely to pay (assuming they have the money) and the higher your potential profitability. Therefore, analyze your value proposition by evaluating the price customers will pay relative to their alternatives, as well as the benefits they will receive. When the benefits are more easily quantifiable, as they often are in capital equipment sold to large companies, it is easier to calculate the value proposition. But with consumers, you have the added nonfinancial factors such as social benefits that cannot be easily quantified. You may need to test to find these to get a better perception of the value proposition to your customers.

Quicken dominated the field of tax software by understanding its value proposition. The penetration rate for tax software was low until Quicken realized that its customers were still using paper forms to file their income tax returns due to the complexity of the software. By making the basic software simple, Quicken attracted taxpayers looking to file basic tax returns and soared to dominance.[1]

Focusing On the Right Uses and Motives Helps to Decide the Best Marketing Mix

Understanding how customers use your product allows you to improve on current marketing strategies and to find expansion opportunities through new products and market segments. Therefore, define your product or service not only in terms of what you are selling but why people are buying, and use that to develop your plan to grow by satisfying customer needs. Customers' motivations can include any combination of the following:

- Economic, which can include financial issues such as total costs, financial benefits, and maintenance issues

- Functional, which includes attributes such as size, speed, etc.

- Physical, which includes motives such as shelter, food, and nutrition

- Psychological, which includes intangible needs, such as prestige; perception of change (which can be an opportunity or threat); and the personal risk to the decision maker

- Social, which can include peer group and family influence, feedback from reference groups, social class, and culture

Jill Blashack Strahan started Tastefully Simple to sell gourmet foods using the home-party strategy because she found that her customers liked to get together, have fun, and taste gourmet foods. So she built her business around fun, food, and parties into a giant in the food industry with an investment of under $25,000.[2]

If You Cannot Differentiate in Your Product, Do It in the Business

How your product(s) compares with its competitors can have major implications for your business. If all the products are similar, the other companies are more established, and you are not offering any unique benefits, customers may not switch to you. You may need to differentiate yourself elsewhere to grow.

Michael Dell started his company to sell personal computers—just like hundreds of other entrepreneurs at the time. His differentiation was to sell them directly to consumers and businesses and to customize the PC for each customer. This differentiation helped him build a direct-selling business model to sell customized PCs and added billions to his net worth.

DIFFERENTIATE TO DOMINATE AN UNTAPPED SEGMENT

If your new product is competing with established competitors in established markets, your product (A in Figure 9) is better on the key variable that encourages customers to switch to you, and you can maintain this advantage (via patents, etc.), then you have a good chance of success.

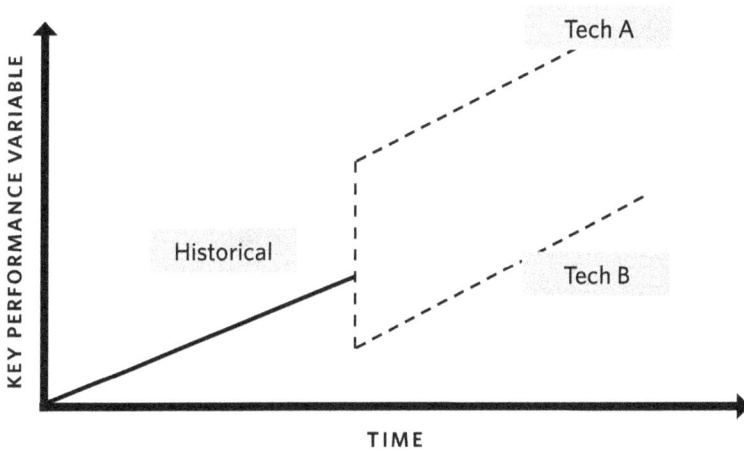

Figure 9. Strategy based on benefits from a technology advance

But what if you have a new technology (B) that is worse on today's key performance variable that is valued by customers but is better on a second variable that may not be highly valued by today's key markets? This is often the issue with revolutionary technologies. In such a case, the new technology may have to find a new market that may be today's fringe market but is more open to your uniqueness. The venture can get a foothold in this fringe market, while continuously improving the technology to become more competitive in the key performance variable. When it does, the venture may be able to dominate other market segments.

When Akio Morita of Sony introduced his transistor radio, the sound was not as good as some of the furniture-type radios that were popular then. But the portability appealed to teenagers—many of whom wanted to listen to Elvis.

Similarly, the early PCs were toys, their power was unimpressive compared with the mainframes of the day, and they were mainly used for playing games. However, when the right software was developed, PCs offered independent computing capacity, and many financial analysts started using them for spreadsheets and financial statements. As PCs became more powerful, they took over the lucrative corporate computing market and destroyed the large mainframe computer manufacturers.

UNDERSTANDING YOUR MARKET HELPS YOU TO DIFFERENTIATE AND ACHIEVE DEMAND-PULL

Two important ways to develop a successful business from scratch include supply-push, where you develop a product or service and hope that customers buy, and demand-pull, where you find unmet needs and develop a better solution. Supply-push works well when you have developed a great marketing campaign to convince customers to buy your product. Many consumer products in mature industries fall into this category. Demand-pull works well when you have a terrific new technology that can solve customers' unmet needs better than existing solutions. As an example, a cure for cancer will have a strong demand. The greater the value, the more customers will pay, if they can afford it.

Mark Knudson of Venturi Group, who has developed many hit companies in the medical device industry, works backward. He first identifies a billion-dollar market and then develops a product that more than satisfies the unmet need to create demand-pull. He has built five successful companies following this formula.[3]

Michael Bloomberg left Salomon Brothers with $10 million and the goal to make traders more productive and profitable. His terminal, which has been called "the iPhone for Wall Street," allowed traders to get real-time data, calculate the value of financial assets under various scenarios, and communicate with others. Traders using his product were more productive. This meant that Bloomberg could charge more, and customers were willing to pay a premium. By knowing how to make his customers happier, he was able to build Bloomberg LP and amassed one of the world's great fortunes.[4]

FIND YOUR ENTRY WEDGE IN STEALTH MODE

Billion-dollar entrepreneurs started their businesses with capital-efficiency. They did not succeed because they spent a fortune on advertising and promotion. They first spent time in stealth mode to find their differentiation—the right wedge—for dominance. They invested heavily only after they found this wedge and reached Aha. At this time, they could raise less-expensive financing from financiers who did not demand control.

Don Kotula launched Northern Tool with his own savings, promoted his first products with pinpoint marketing in "he-man" publications, sold (rather than offering for free) the instruction booklet to assemble his first product, used targeted direct mail to sell additional products, and then launched stores in targeted areas based on the location of existing customers.[5]

Horst Rechelbacher used his skills in hairdressing and photography to launch his pioneering organic line of beauty products for his Aveda brand. He did it without a public relations budget by learning how to publicize his company and his products.[6]

• • •

Your entry could make you or break you. Find the right wedge and you could get customers quickly with a low cost of sales and marketing and with high margins. You could take off with low levels of capital. Without such a wedge, you could run out of cash and out of runway before your venture takes off.

CHAPTER 16

Grow with the Segment from Heaven

Can you find the segment of customers who are such a perfect fit for your product or service that they are easy to reach, buy immediately, pay more, keep buying from you, and tell all their friends, who also buy from you? That is a segment from heaven. Find yours, and you can get established immediately and grow fast with value.

"Find the customers from heaven and avoid the ones from hell to improve your odds of success."

—Dileep Rao

A segment is a group of potential customers with similar characteristics, ability, and motivation to buy the product and at a high price. Successful entrepreneurs focus on the one right customer segment. Trying to market a new product to all potential customer segments is likely to result in a lack of focus and create competitive weakness. An entrepreneur seeking to dominate two segments is likely to be at a disadvantage against others who focus on one segment, all other things being equal. Even Walmart focuses on its key target segment and does not try to be all things to all people. That is because each segment is likely to need a unique combination of product, service, pricing, marketing strategy, and positioning, and it is extremely difficult and expensive to reach and convince different types of segments.

Eight years after starting Walmart, Sam Walton took the company public. With a debt-free balance sheet, he started to expand. What he found was that Kmart was not going to towns of fewer than 50,000. And he knew that his own formula could succeed in all sizes of towns and did very well in towns of fewer than even 5,000 people. So that is where he focused. He used his plane to fly over small towns, scout the locations and traffic flows, check up on the competitors, and pick the best site. Because truckers would not supply him in many of these small towns, he set up his own distribution system, which added to his competitive advantage. And he found that America had "plenty of those towns out there" for Walmart's expansion.[1]

To focus on the right segment, you first need to understand the various types of customers, their needs, and how they can be grouped. Then pick the one whose unmet needs match your competitive edge.

Why You Should Focus on the Segment from Heaven

By dividing customers into market segments, entrepreneurs can develop focused strategies to dominate the right segment. Customer segmentation can be one of the most important aspects of your business model.

FOCUS TO DOMINATE

Billion-dollar entrepreneurs focus on the segment that they can dominate. Successful companies know their best segment—the best group of customers, who have the motivation to buy the product (or service), the purchasing power to pay a higher price, and the potential loyalty to help the company dominate. If the group is also a high-growth, high-potential segment, that is an added advantage.

Focusing on the right group of customers makes it easier to dominate with capital-efficiency.

FOCUS BECAUSE YOUR COST OF MONEY IS HIGH AND AVAILABILITY IS LOW

In the early stages, your cost of money is high. Professional VCs seek annual returns as high as 80 to 100 percent for companies at the research and development stage, and most will not even consider financing before you have a product or service already developed. Raising money from professional VCs at this stage will require that you give up control of the venture and of the wealth that the venture may create, assuming you can get VC. So focus your scarce resources on the most attractive segment where your competitive advantage fits their unmet need, and dominate it. Identify and separate the "leaders and the bleeders," that is, those who should lead your priority list of customers and those who will bleed you because they are not the right customers for you. Focusing on the leaders should allow you to improve your sales and margins in a shorter time period and at lower cost. Avoiding bleeders should help you cut waste.

Don Kotula focused on the "he-man" do-it-yourself market. He targets males who like to use various kinds of tools and equipment, and he has built his chain of stores, Northern Tool, into nearly a billion-dollar company around their needs.

Similarly, Bob Kierlin focused on manufacturers and contractors to build Fastenal, and Jill Blashack Strahan focused on women who like to try gourmet foods in a party atmosphere.

FOCUS TO BETTER SATISFY SEGMENT NEEDS AND DOMINATE WITH A PROPRIETARY ADVANTAGE

Segments have unique needs. It is usually easier for a newer venture to develop the one right mix of product, price, package, distribution, and promotion to better satisfy one segment's key unmet needs than scattering its attention and resources on a wide variety of customer segments. Focusing should help you to direct your resources to satisfy the segment's needs, improve your market share, and dominate the segment.

Dell Computer initially focused on customers who wanted, and were willing, to buy customized PCs directly from the company by direct mail. By selling to this segment, Dell gained other advantages, such as being able to customize the product for each customer, buy parts after receiving the order and the payment to cut inventory, and use just-in-time manufacturing for higher profit margins.

FOCUS TO FIND THE RIGHT SALES AND DISTRIBUTION CHANNELS

Sales and distribution channels can impact (1) the venture, due to their impact on the level of sales; (2) the net revenues, after discounts to distributors and retailers, commissions, and other costs to get sales; and (3) the time lag from spending on marketing to revenue collection, which creates the need for financing. Types of channels can include the following:

- Direct to businesses: It is easier for a new venture to sell directly to large businesses, assuming that the larger businesses are not reluctant to buy from new ventures.

- Direct to local consumers: This can be via company stores or franchises, which can require substantial investments in the local store to reach a small market (but one that can be replicated in other markets).

- Direct to national consumer market: This strategy is usually difficult for undercapitalized new ventures. The Internet has allowed new ventures to succeed with direct sales to national (or global) consumers and created giants such as Amazon.com. But this strategy can still need significant levels of capital to dominate.

- Direct to governments: The key problem with selling to governments is that most value low prices. This means that they may not pay more for high-value products. Many governments are also corrupt.

- Indirect channels: Indirect channels, such as using distributors and retailers, can be expensive to organize and cost more in the form of discounts and promotion expenses. But these channels can be used to reach a wider audience, assuming that the larger market will buy from you and you have the financing to sell to them.

FOCUS TO DOMINATE

Domination helps. Dominating a market segment allows you to control pricing and profits. Dominating an emerging market may be one of the best strategies for entrepreneurial growth because emerging markets don't have entrenched competitors, and they could take off. It is difficult to make a frontal assault against better-entrenched competitors in more mature markets. Most billion-dollar entrepreneurs jumped on an emerging trend or dominated fragmented industries and did not directly compete against larger competitors. So if you are going to enter a large existing market, first find a fragmented one and then become better than the competitors. And if the industry is an oligopoly and not fragmented, seek to dominate niche markets, especially when the large elephants are grazing in the bigger fields.

When his large employer closed its Minnesota operations, Eric Paulson realized that he could become a local distributor for music and software and help retailers headquartered locally to better manage their operations. This is what he was doing for his employer. And the fact that some of the nation's large retailers were in Minneapolis helped Paulson. He opened his business with a warehouse, nothing to sell, and no one to sell to. The key to getting started was to be able to convince record labels that he could be a better distributor than the ones they currently used and to convince retailers that he could give them great service. He positioned himself as the only independent distributor in Minnesota, since the closest warehouse was in Chicago. Being the only local distributor, the retailers could get immediate access to products to replenish their shelves. This meant more turns and better inventory control. This was his niche. He signed up all the local retailers, including Musicland, Target, and Dart Records. And with his connections to the music industry, he signed up a dozen labels. He made a profit in the first year.[2]

Paul Orfalea built Kinko's into a national copying chain and sold it to FedEx for $2.4 billion by focusing on his niche—college students. While visiting the University of California, Santa Barbara, Orfalea noticed that there was no copy shop close by that could serve the student community. He knew from his own experience that students needed copies, and he opened his first copy shop in a hamburger store. The hamburger shop was near UCSB and attracted traffic. Orfalea's advertising was a board outside the shop.[3]

· · ·

By focusing on your best customer segments, you can target your resources to satisfy their needs better than your competitors, dominate these segments, and sustain your competitive advantage.

CHAPTER 17

Target the Right Strategic Group to Dominate and Grow

Can you find a strategic group that is smaller, newer, and weaker, while growing faster than the overall industry? That is usually the case in emerging industries until someone finds the key to unlocking an advantage. Or you might find an industry that is fragmented with smaller competitors and potentially easier to dominate if you can find the advantage. Many entrepreneurs target markets. Targeting competitors may be just as fruitful.

"Pick the pond where you can become the biggest frog and then expand the size of the pond."

—Dileep Rao

Consider Bill Gates, Steve Jobs, Michael Dell, Mark Zuckerberg, Jeff Bezos, Bob Kierlin, and many other billion-dollar entrepreneurs. They dominated their strategic group. They just happened to dominate the strategic group that was seeking to take advantage of a potential multibillion-dollar emerging industry.

In a fight, it is usually easier to win against someone who is smaller, weaker, and less smart than you are. The same is true in business. It is not enough to find the right customers. You also need to find the right direct competitors, that is, your strategic group. These are the ones selling to the same customers and often in the same way as you. Beat them and you dominate your market. Dominate your market and you build value.

Your strategic group includes your direct competitors that are targeting the same customers. Ideally, you should be able to enter a high-growth strategic group with low barriers to entry, erect barriers after you enter, and dominate the group. As the VCs say, you need to be at the "center of a hot flame."

Understanding your direct and indirect competition helps you to determine and develop your sustained competitive advantage to dominate your strategic group. Highly successful companies have a sustainable advantage. This advantage does not have to be based on a patent, although patents can be helpful. Entrepreneurs have used a variety of strategies to dominate. In addition to unique technologies, companies can excel at strategies such as controlling the core product, such as Microsoft did, or using new channels, such as Amazon.com, or using new trends, such as Chipotle.

Walmart selected the right location. When Sam Walton was expanding across rural America, his direct competitors were mainly small merchants who could not win against his juggernaut. What is amazing is that no one else duplicated this business model before he built an impregnable business. Kmart tried to enter rural markets, but it was too little, too late.

THINKING YOU HAVE NO COMPETITION IS DANGEROUS

It's very important to pick the right strategic group. Many entrepreneurs seek innovations where they have "no competition." In reality, it is good to have competition in new ventures because it proves that there is a market. Every business has competition, unless there is no need. To succeed, you need to be better than your competition. If you truly have no competitors, the need may not exist or it may be latent and you may have to create the need. This can be expensive and time consuming. Not many entrepreneurs have the resources to do this.

THE RIGHT GROUP WITH A GROWING GROUP-SHARE CAN GIVE YOU AN ADVANTAGE AGAINST INDIRECT COMPETITORS

In general, it is beneficial to be in an emerging, strategic group that has significant competitive advantages over well-entrenched, indirectly competing groups. With the advantage of a revolutionary technology or some other key advantage such as a new business model, the strategic group could be gaining "group-share" over the other groups, and can help you grow. So determine the strengths, weaknesses, and trends of your strategic group versus the indirect competitors.

Joining the right group that had a growing group-share helped several companies, from Sam Walton, who joined the big box retailers when they were spreading, to Gates and Jobs, who joined the emerging PC industry, to Zuckerberg and Bezos, who became part of the expanding group of companies that have exploited the Internet.

EMERGING INDUSTRIES OFFER THE POTENTIAL OF HIGH GROWTH

Emerging industries offer high potential. Seventy-eight percent of the high-performance entrepreneurs in Minnesota, and 42 percent of the billion-dollar entrepreneurs in the national group, were in emerging industries. VCs seek to enter high-growth, emerging industries where they can invest capital for fast growth and erect barriers. An industry with low barriers to entry is attractive for entrepreneurs without capital. Examples of high barriers include the need for an expensive-to-develop marketing presence or distribution channel, or the ongoing need for expensive research and development. The latter type of venture needs to raise money. But if the money is not available or if the cost is too high, you need to find strategies with low barriers and then erect barriers by developing sticky relationships with your customers so they don't leave.

Emerging industries have been one of the biggest drivers of growth for billion-dollar entrepreneurs. The success stories include Intel in semiconductors, Apple in PCs, Cisco in telecom, Google in search, and Chipotle in organic food. These companies used the benefits offered by new technologies or new trends to join an emerging strategic group and profit.

SEEK FRAGMENTED INDUSTRIES OR NICHES IN MATURE ONES

Mature industries can be oligopolistic, with a few large companies, or they can be fragmented and have many small, weaker companies. Entering monopolistic or oligopolistic markets, where one or a few companies dominate, can be tough. In oligopolistic industries, ventures often serve niche markets not served by established companies, especially until the venture is able to establish a foothold.

Capella University focused on distance-based graduate programs because Apollo, the industry giant, was focusing on the larger undergraduate education market at that time. The graduate education market was underserved, and Capella's customers already had good study habits from their undergraduate days. As a result, Capella was able to spend less on hand-holding with its students.

Elon Musk started Tesla in a niche of the auto industry that was dominated by giants by focusing on cars powered by batteries.

Lloyd Sigel built Lloyd's Barbeque to dominance in the frozen, precooked meat section of the grocery market, which was an industry controlled by giants. He noticed that women had less time since they were working outside the home, and new technologies to pack precooked meat were available. He combined the two trends to build a giant company. And then he sold it to an even larger giant.

Fragmented industries can be attractive to entrepreneurs, due to the potential of weaker competition and the availability of more options. The billion-dollar entrepreneurs who were not in emerging industries were mostly in fragmented industries with weaker competitors. It may be easier to dominate the weaker competitors in a fragmented industry, especially if you have an advantage in your technology, strategy, financial strength, or leadership capacity. Entering a strategic group where your direct competitors are weaker may help you get big and dominate.

Ray Kroc of McDonald's, a pioneer in the quick-serve food industry, competed against small restaurants and dominated by franchising. They did not have the resources, national and global presence, and ability to implement sophisticated marketing strategies.

When entrepreneurs such as Michael Dell entered the PC industry, there were hundreds of vendors selling PCs. He decided to focus on direct selling, a strategy that was used by few.

Dick Schulze opened three stores to sell consumer electronics when there were thousands of competitors. He dominated the industry when he joined the big-store trend and became the best and the biggest.

Bob Kierlin started a store called Fastenal to sell nuts and bolts in a very fragmented industry. The barriers to entry were low. He then used his leadership skills to dominate the industry.

BEING IN THE RIGHT GROUP CAN ATTRACT GREAT PARTNERS

Sometimes your competitors can become your customers if you know how both can benefit. Find their pain and reduce it to form alliances in your industry.

Bonnie Baskin built ViroMed and AppTec, two biotech companies, when the industry was emerging. She sold them for around $203 million. To perform diagnostics on viruses, Baskin had to have living cells for the viruses to thrive. There were two companies on the East Coast that provided the cells—fresh monkey kidney cells—each week. For Baskin, the minimum order was more than she would need. So she found the manager at a local hospital who was going to start an in-house lab. Baskin called him and offered to sell him a part of her purchase of the monkey cells. He agreed to let Baskin buy the cells, process them, and sell the final product to him. This cell product division grew to include over 25 types of cells and became a multimillion-dollar national business. ViroMed became a clinical testing laboratory for hospitals and also a supplier of the raw materials to testing labs.[1]

• • •

Pick the right competitors. Then become better than them. To do this, pick emerging industries to compete with newer companies that are also growing. Or choose fragmented industries where it is easy to enter and where it is easier to beat the other small companies if you have a competitive edge or a trend at your back. As Rechelbacher (Aveda) said, "At first, competitors think you'll fail. Later they know they will fail."

CHAPTER 18

Developing Value in Your Strategy

Technologists often believe that all they have to do is build a great product, and it will sell itself, especially with viral marketing. Unless you are incredibly lucky, that never happens because most products can be imitated. To obtain a long-term advantage, it helps to develop an advantage in your business strategy.

"Develop value and sell value for long-term advantage to charge more, sell more, and keep more."

—Dileep Rao

Imitation allows for fast entry. But, except in emerging industries where all the companies are learning the market, its unmet needs, and the fulcrum that can give you an advantage, imitation alone does not add value. In emerging industries, the demand could outstrip the supply and make entry easier. But when the markets mature, or when one company gets an edge, you could lose out unless you add value. And without added value, you could be growth and profit challenged. You could try a price war, but the strongest, usually entrenched competitors, will win.

If established competitors let you grab customers because they are snoozing, you may be able to establish a beachhead. But you have to be lucky.

Hamdi Ulukaya started a yogurt company called Chobani.[1] His larger competitors did not take him or his Greek yogurt seriously, until he had built a large company.

Tony Hsieh funded and then became CEO of Zappos. Initially, Zappos had shoes shipped by manufacturers directly to customers. But as the company grew, Hsieh found that he needed to control the entire customer experience to add value and happiness. He "had to give up the easy money, manage the inventory, and take the risk."[2]

Billion-dollar entrepreneurs, especially if they are capital-smart, usually enter fragmented or emerging industries due to ease of entry, and they have plenty of competitors due to low barriers of entry. To stand out from the crowd, they need to become sticky with their customers by adding value.

When You Offer More Value, You Can Charge More

Industries have their high performers and their low performers. Usually new ventures do not have the size to be efficient. They succeed by adding value and by attracting customers who pay more, which makes them more profitable and helps their growth.

According to Aveda's Rechelbacher, to excel at hair design, you first must practice to master the technical details. Next, you copy the masters to know their techniques. Then you improve on them to win.

Gary Holmes is one of the biggest real estate developers in Minnesota. When he started buying properties (at age 14, from the profits of a business selling light bulbs that he founded at age 11), he found that there were three types of problem units that were attributable to the owners. In the first, the landlord offered a discount on the rent for any problems and told the renters to fix them. In the second, owners never fixed up the units, even with such simple improvements as painting and other minor cosmetics. To compensate, they kept rents low. A third kind did not know the level of market rents since they had not checked and done their homework. Holmes learned that if he bought these underperforming units and improved the management, he could get more rent and improve his margins. This was the start of his real-estate empire.[3]

DEVELOP VALUE, BECAUSE CUSTOMERS NEVER BEAT A PATH TO YOUR DOOR

Technologists often believe that all they have to do is build a great product and it will sell itself, or that they can rely on viral marketing. Unless you are incredibly lucky, that never happens. You have to seek customers and convince them of how you can solve their unmet needs, and then convince them to buy from you.

Even a game-changing, life-enhancing product, like the Medtronic cardiac pacemaker, had to be sold. With the introduction of the pacemaker, Medtronic had to use missionary zeal and every available and effective means to promote its products. Cofounders Earl Bakken and Palmer Hermundslie realized that technology was not enough. Since the pacemaker was such a revolutionary technology, customers did not always know what the product was, or how it could meet their needs. Credibility and trust were key. Credibility is crucial when selling any product, especially one involving human life. Bakken and his partner found that it was not easy to convince the conservative medical establishment to use their pacemakers to treat their patients. However, when leading physicians presented their groundbreaking advances with Medtronic pacemakers at surgical conferences, other physicians would listen and start to use their products. They were obviously willing to listen to leaders in their own profession but not to entrepreneurs trying to "sell" them a product.

• • •

Without value, pricing cannot be high. This translates to lower margins, making high profitability and growth difficult.

CHAPTER 19

Price for Value, Growth, and Cash Flow

Pricing is one of the most important aspects of your business strategy. Many entrepreneurs instinctively want to be "cheaper." This could be the worst mistake you could make. Price affects everything, especially success. Most high-performance, billion-dollar and hundred-million-dollar entrepreneurs grew with higher prices. But the first question is, how do you measure "high" or "low"?

> "Price affects everything, especially success."
>
> **—Dileep Rao**

Pricing is perhaps the most important decision you will make. Pricing affects your revenues, profits, cash flow, asset needs, financing, and financial needs. Pricing affects the company's culture, and it influences the customers' perception of your products or service and of your company, especially when it is not easy for them to compare value. Price too high and customers may buy if they think you offer high value, or they might think you are overpriced and not buy, or you may attract competition. Price too low and you may not cover costs and fail even if you get sales, or your offering may be perceived as a "discount" product and attract unwanted customers. Finding the right price is not easy, but it is important.

Pricing Higher

Pricing higher than direct competitors or seeking high margins often results in lower sales, unless customers value high prices and buy more at higher prices. This can be the case with some products and services where perception is key. But usually higher prices need added value—or the perception of added value. Price high if you are able to sell value to your customers. The lower unit sales that are likely to result from higher pricing may also mean that you need fewer assets and have lower financing needs.

Tom Auth built ITI into a giant in the wireless security alarm industry. As the pioneer in this industry, ITI made it unnecessary to wire homes. This saved money and time for the installers, who could install many homes in the same time that it took to wire one. Auth, however, charged more for his technology and kept the installers' savings for himself. His installers kept the lifetime value of each new installation because customers seldom changed vendors when security systems were wired.

When Gustavo Cisneros (cofounder of Univision) was introducing DirecTV to Latin America, his segmentation strategy was to focus on rich neighborhoods that did not have access to cable TV. These were customers who were ready to pay a premium price for a better product. And Cisneros also did not want to get into a price war with Rupert Murdoch's Sky TV.[1]

While all customers have a strong focus on price, it is not the only focus. You can charge higher prices if the customers are not price sensitive, or when you add significant value to justify the higher price, such as better availability, location, delivery, quality, service, image, or exclusivity. To add value, develop your edge based on your customers' real needs. You need to find out what they really want and where they will happily pay more, then offer the level of quality, service, and timeliness that customers seek. That gets you higher margins and profits.

Most food companies had their plants in the eastern half of the nation when Glenn Hasse was starting his business because that is where most consumers were located. Hasse built his food outsourcing giant in Minnesota, which was farther away from the markets. So he decided that he would compete not on price, but on his commitment to provide quality, service, and speed. Companies in the food industry worry about the quality of the product to avoid any harm to their brand. These companies also place a high importance on the level of service to them and to the supply chain, and the timeliness of deliveries to avoid stock-outs. Not having product on the shelves, especially when a promotion is going on, is devastating. Hasse focused his attention on these variables.

To price higher, add value. Pricing lower can be dangerous for new companies, especially if you are settling for lower quality and standards to be able to charge less. There is nearly always someone bigger and cheaper than you. You may get sales but not profits, and you may end up in a price war where the strongest win. To succeed, learn how to compete with higher standards of quality and service and how to sell this higher value.

Jill Blashack Strahan worked for Jan Strauss, her high school teacher and advisor who was opening a tanning salon, before she started and built Tastefully Simple, a giant in gourmet foods. There was another tanning studio in the local market, and Strauss's strategy was to offer a newer facility with better equipment, an excellent brand, and higher standards of customer service, and to charge a higher price—$6, versus $5 per tan at the older salon. This concept was new to Blashack Strahan, who was used to seeing businesses compete with lower prices. Strauss installed timers so the tanning session would end at a prearranged time, rather than relying on someone pounding on the wall. Her business offered fresh towels, headsets, bigger tanning beds, and cooler rooms in a new building. Her tanning salon became so popular that it had more than 100 clients in a day and started to show a profit in less than one year.

Pricing Lower

Many entrepreneurs think they can offer higher quality and better service at a lower price to get new customers. Often a lower price conveys the opposite of what is intended. Price low and you could give the perception that your products are of poor quality. Remember, customers may believe in the old saying that "you get what you pay for."

As a smaller or newer venture, your costs may also be higher than those of your established competitors. And higher unit sales from the lower prices may need more assets and financing but without the margins or cash flow to pay lenders or offer an attractive return to investors. And if your lower prices do not get you a commensurate higher volume, you may show negative income and cash flow. Perhaps worst of all, you may have captured a market segment that is attracted by your low prices and may disappear when you try to raise them.

Netflix lost a significant portion of its customers and its market capitalization when it abruptly tried to increase prices, and it was forced to back down. Netflix has obviously learned from its mistakes and is doing a gradual price increase.[2]

Lower prices are not a great option for new ventures that are competing with established businesses and hope that lower prices will get market share. If the large, existing competitors can survive with lower prices for a longer time than you can, due to their deeper pockets or the ability to match your edge, you might not be able to sustain your business.

In commodity-type businesses where you have no product or technology advantage, a lower price may draw customers if price is key, if it is easy to compare your product (and service) with the competition, and if customers see that your lower price does not connote lower quality and service, or they are willing to live with the lower quality. But be sure that you are not starting a price war that you cannot win. To successfully compete on price, you also should be the low-cost leader, which normally needs high market share or a new business model.

Jim Sinegal built Costco in the emerging warehouse-store industry into a nearly $100 billion business by emphasizing lower prices. He used the business model of big-box, warehouse-style stores, with customers having to buy memberships to encourage their loyalty. In turn, he was loyal to them. Even when he could raise prices and charge more for his products (including Costco's Kirkland Signature private label), he did not. He kept his markups constant at 14 percent for non-Kirkland products and at 15 percent for Kirkland products. This had the dual results of making his customers happier and making his competitors less competitive.[3]

For most entrepreneurs, lower prices are a one-way ticket to failure, because entrenched competitors often can win a price war with more resources and with customers who stick to them.

Glen Taylor built his wedding-invitation printing business into the largest in the country by being competitive with standard products but offering upgrades such as color-coordinated paper. He was the first wedding-invitation printer to go to the New York bridal shows to find out the next year's color trend, which he then ordered from his paper manufacturer to match the bridal designs. He also offered better service by incorporating a variety of small improvements, such as using UPS rather than the USPS. Taylor also improved productivity to become more efficient and to stay competitive in the industry.

Pricing the Same

Price the same and your customers may think you are no different from your competitors. So if you have the same prices as your competitors, you need to find a unique way to differentiate yourself and beat competitors who may have larger marketing budgets. And unless you can show you are adding value, your targeted customers may not switch over to you, forcing you to lower prices to get customers.

Lowering prices to get customers could lead to a price war, which is usually dangerous for the newer business.

Value Influences Price

Entrepreneurs normally face a higher cost structure when they start. They can bootstrap to reduce their overhead and fixed costs but, since their sales levels are low, their per-unit costs are quite high. As noted in Table 7, this means that entrepreneurs need to add value so they can price high and attain a reasonable margin, or find a way to cut costs and add value to survive with a lower price and high cost structure.

TABLE 7. THE VALUE-COST-PRICE MATRIX

Customer value high	Price high to low	Price high for value and to cover cost
Customer value low	Price low	Cut costs, add value or exit
	Low Cost Structure	High Cost Structure

When he started Amazon.com, Jeff Bezos was selling books in competition with giants such as Borders and Barnes & Noble. Since the books were the same, he had to find a way to compete. By selling solely on the Internet, Bezos could sell for less since he did not have the fixed overhead of bookstores. The fact that books could be bought in small quantities, and unsold copies could be returned, also helped Bezos compete with the giants. With a lower cost structure, he could sell for less. But he used one of the most disruptive technologies of the last century, the Internet.

Pricing should depend upon a number of factors. The floor should be influenced by cost and the ceiling by customer value. The value proposition to the customer is a function of the additional value they can get from your product or service compared with the value they can get from alternative choices.

Glen Taylor was able to achieve higher margins for his wedding invitations by offering customized cards. Previously, cards were affiliated with religious denominations. He offered cards based on the current pop hits in music and movies. Previously, Taylor's cards came only in standard colors because he had to order paper in large quantities. Taylor started offering cards in colors that matched the bridal dresses, and he had to push these colors to brides. He found that when brides could express their personality in their cards, they did not worry about prices. He ended up dominating the industry.

Howard Schultz of Starbucks was able to charge over $2 for a cup of coffee by changing the concept of coffee from a drink to an occasion. Customers could linger in coffee bars, as they do in Italy, and "pamper" themselves with a latte.[4]

The first instinct of many entrepreneurs is to price lower for a competitive edge. The better way to price is based on perceived value to the customer. Understand what your customers want, know your competition, and know the competitive value you offer. Then *know how to sell value and set your price to value.*

Richard Burke (UnitedHealth) faced the pricing problem when he was managing one of the early health maintenance organizations (HMOs). The HMO had thousands of unrelated physicians as owners and service providers, and they did not want to cut their prices. Burke and his staff turned what seemed a disadvantage into a competitive advantage. Burke found an opportunity to charge a premium price by offering patients access to more medical providers, and especially to retain their existing physicians. He was also able to avoid the need for claim forms, and reduced other administrative headaches. This strategy generated higher revenues and was the keystone to Burke's success. The HMOs managed by Burke became financially stronger. There was more money available to pay the doctors, which made them happier, and they became ambassadors for the services of Burke's firm elsewhere. The improved pricing model turned around the fortunes of the HMO almost overnight, so that Burke's firm had its successful prototype to exhibit to similar physician groups elsewhere in the country.

PRICING INFLUENCES YOUR CUSTOMER SEGMENT

Each customer segment has its own price-value requirements. Customers who value convenience and higher levels of service usually expect to pay higher prices. The others can get a discount and accept lower levels of service. This is evident, for example, in the pricing strategies of airlines and the way they price their seats.

When the quick-oil-change concept was new, Ed Flaherty (Rapid Oil Change) had to determine the premium his customers were willing to pay. He offered a discount program for his price-sensitive customers who could wait, thus allowing him to show a marked differentiation between his two price levels. Rapid Oil Change had positive cash flow from month one. Each store had positive cash flow, and Flaherty made sure that he only went into locations where he knew he could develop cash flow immediately. Flaherty first analyzed competitors' prices. He realized that *many customers were willing to pay up to twice as much as the "loss leader" prices that his competitors sometimes promoted.* He used loss-leader pricing only to get the marginal customer who could come in during slow periods.

PRICING AFFECTS YOUR COMPETITIVE ADVANTAGE

Know how you will make money. In retail, allow consumers to compare prices where you are competitive. This practice is prevalent in all the so-called "discount" retailers. But learn how to charge higher prices elsewhere by developing your competitive advantage. Lower pricing in one area draws customers. Higher pricing elsewhere draws profits.

Harold Roitenberg (who built a $6 billion retail chain called Modern Merchandising) realized that he had a knack for merchandising because he understood his customers, their needs, and knew his competitive advantage. His customers wanted top name brands, such as Nikon cameras, at lower prices. Often he would price the top name-brand cameras at below-market prices as sales leaders. He would then sell high-margin jewelry to these customers. It was easy for the customers to check prices of name-brand items, such as appliances, cameras, and electronics. Lower prices in this area helped create the perception of a low-priced catalog and helped sell jewelry at higher margins.[5]

• • •

Pricing is one of the most important aspects of a venture. Price lower and you may get higher revenues with lower profits and higher financing needs. And you could get into a price war. Most high-performance entrepreneurs priced high or high-low, where low prices were their marketing tool, but they knew how to get customers to buy higher-margin products.

CHAPTER 20

Prove Your Strategy: Fail Small, Win Big

There is no shortage of entrepreneurs with dreams. There is a shortage of ventures with proven potential. Sophisticated investors seek proof of potential before investing. To prove your strategy, test to fail small and win big.

> "If you go too fast, you can lose money. We push on the accelerator only when everything is in place."
>
> **—Bernard Arnault, CEO, LVMH**[1]

Uncertainty is one of the biggest hurdles in a new business. There is no history to rely on when you are developing a new business. You do not know which strategy will work. You do not know which product will be best, which customer segment to target, which competitive advantage to focus on, which sales driver to use, what the actual sales or profits will be, and the answers to hundreds of similar questions that can affect the success of your venture.

There are many factors that influence eventual success, including the right product, the right strategy, the right timing and speed, and the right people. Maintaining a reasonable level of humility helps entrepreneurs remember that they don't have all the answers, that they don't predict accurately all the time, that customers don't always show up on time and in sufficient numbers, and if they think they know it all, they will soon find out that they do not. Companies that developed flat-screen TVs, Unix software, and the laser printer were not the ones that eventually profited from the technology. Innovation alone is not enough, and a product's potential is not always obvious until someone proves that demand for it exists. You need to pick the right opportunity to pursue. And you need to pick the right strategy. And you need to do this before you run out of money. Test first to reduce losses.

About 50 percent of all new businesses are said to fail within five years, and 71 percent fail within 10.[2] About 80 percent of all venture capital investments fail to offer the desired returns. This means that even professionals make mistakes. You can use your instinct to make decisions, but instinct is another word for guessing. Call it instinct or call it scientific guessing, it is still guessing. Sometimes you may be forced to guess, especially when you have to react immediately. But in situations without the pressure of immediacy, billion-dollar entrepreneurs did not guess. They tested before they moved forward because they knew that instinct can be fallible. Instinct may be good for generating ideas, but it is not a good tool to decide what to do and how to do it. Everyone has instincts, and many act on them. That's why so many fail.

Why Test?

Successful entrepreneurs want to make sure that they are using assumptions that are real and that their instincts are tested.

INSTINCT CAN BE WRONG—IT IS ANOTHER WORD FOR GUESSING

Idea generation is easy. Business development is hard. New businesses do not have the luxury of experience, so they must develop policies from scratch. Entrepreneurs must make many decisions as they start and build their businesses. Using instinct can easily lead to losses. Established businesses evaluate the real, tested results from their experience and codify them as policies. Testing can be time consuming and slower—but it can help the venture find its growth opportunity.

When Richard Branson started Virgin Atlantic Airways, he knew that he could lose it all. So he started out by leasing one plane for a short term of one year. Unfortunately, this did not account for the unexpected: A bird got sucked into one of the engines, and Branson had not insured the plane. He had to siphon cash from his record company and leverage his airline. He then ran into turbulence from British Airways, before winning a lawsuit. All of this left him financially drained, and he had to sell Virgin Records to invest in Virgin Atlantic.[3]

When should entrepreneurs use instinct, if ever, and when should they test? In general, to avoid disasters, operate on data.

To broaden its toy product line, Tonka Toys constantly searched for new toys outside the company because Steve Shank believed that transformative lines come from the outside. The company could license these toys to take advantage of the company's key strength, which was sales and distribution. Shank believed that a hit's potential can be seen early on and that the disasters are also evident in early tests. The key was to *limit instincts to generating ideas and narrowing options but test to reveal what the market wants*. Shank did not invest heavily until tests showed positive results. Tonka tested new toy lines with kids, especially by competitive-cohort testing—testing against other toys in a similar genre, such as action toys for boys. When a line shows promise against its cohorts, according to Shank, the toys start flying off the shelves and "money starts falling from the skies." Shank used *intuition for idea generation and tests for final selection*.[4]

OTHERS MAY NOT BUY YOUR PRODUCT OR BUY INTO YOUR ENTHUSIASM

You must *prove* the potential, especially when seeking partners, customers, and money. Sometimes it is not easy to convince others when all you are using is your intuition.

Dan Cohen (CNS/Breathe Right) developed his major home run in the nasal-strip business. He licensed the strip on an exclusive basis from the developer in return for a 50,000-share option and a royalty of 3 percent. He did not pay any cash, since he could not spare any, but he convinced the inventor that this arrangement would be mutually profitable. However, Cohen's board did not have as favorable a reaction because they did not see any proof of potential success. When board members were informed of Cohen's actions, they suggested that he quit as president to pursue the nasal-strip business since he liked it so much, with the implication that if the strip did not succeed, Cohen would not be working for CNS.

COST OF MONEY VS. RETURN ON MONEY

In the early stages of a venture, the cost of money is high. Due to the high failure rate, VCs often seek annual target returns of 60 to 100 percent for investing in early-stage ventures. While the cost of venture capital falls significantly after the venture is profitable, entrepreneurs need to be careful and test before risking large amounts in the early stages when money is expensive. After the tests are conclusive, and when the risks are lower and the results more predictable, the cost is lower, and entrepreneurs can afford to raise more with less dilution and invest more.

Jeremy Stoppelman built Yelp in the competitive but high-potential local advertising market. Unlike his better-funded new-venture rivals, such as Insider Pages, or his established venture rivals such as Facebook and Google, Stoppelman first concentrated on one market to learn the best way to operate—and make mistakes—in one area. His team invited its best reviewers to join the Yelp Elite Squad and organized parties for them, making it an honor to belong to the group. This improved reviews and offered Yelp a unique strategy to expand without the money that some of his rivals wasted.[5]

BY REDUCING THE MONEY AT RISK, ENTREPRENEURS MAY NOT PULL THE PLUG PREMATURELY

Often the introduction of a revolutionary idea causes a great deal of excitement and optimism. But reality does not always live up to the hype, since those who benefit the most from the new technology may also be conservative and wait for proof of benefit, causing a time lag between the introduction of a revolutionary new idea and its takeoff.[6] Investors and entrepreneurs who expect instant results may be disappointed and exit from the venture, leaving others to share in the rewards when the industry does take off. So go slow, prove the business, and then step on the gas after takeoff.

TEST IN PROPORTION TO THE RISK

You need the right balance between testing to reduce risk and action to take advantage of the opportunity. This means doing the following:

- Understand trends and get secondary data on products, markets, and your direct and indirect competitors.

- Do primary research. Talk to customers. Survey them. Find out what they think and whether they will buy your product.

- Do real research. Find the right customers and ask for the order. Find ways to test whether customers will really buy without customers knowing that you are testing. If your business is selling to consumers, find a way to sell. If you are in retail, open a flash store. If you have a food business, test with a food truck. If you are selling to businesses, see if you can get a contract. If you cannot, maybe the signal is that you are not adding enough value to encourage potential customers to give you a contract. Note that any businesses that give you a conditional contract may ask for some benefits such as lower prices and exclusive benefits.

Testing and Proving the Value of Your Model

What is the right business model for your new business? What should you be selling, to whom, and what are your short- and long-term competitive advantages against your direct and indirect competitors? To reduce your risks and losses, you need to test to find the right one.

Your first business model may not be the one that takes you to dominance. Many entrepreneurs tweak to find the right model to get an edge and pivot when they find it. This is difficult to do in a business plan or via market research, since it needs real-world feedback. After you get into the business for real, you often see opportunities and realities that you would not have seen from the sidelines. So be aware of signals that flash opportunities and warnings. And change if you can to get a long-term advantage.

Bob Kierlin started Fastenal to sell nuts and bolts *using a vending machine.* Two weeks into his venture, he realized that it was a mistake, since customers wanted more varieties of fasteners than could be sold in a vending machine. He switched to a retail store and built the largest fastener firm in the United States.

Emerging industries and mature markets have their own unique issues. In an emerging industry, new competitors are all trying to read and evaluate rapidly changing markets and trends and to find the best way to dominate.

Bill Gates did not start out with the business model that made him rich and famous. Initially, after dropping out of Harvard, he and Paul Allen sold their own line of BASIC software for the Altair 8800.[7] It was only when the company was about five years old, in 1981, that Gates found out that IBM was seeking an operating system for its proposed personal computer line. He bought an operating system from another company in Seattle, called it MS-DOS, licensed it to IBM, and built Microsoft into a juggernaut.

You may not find the right business model on the first cut, so you may have to adapt—before you run out of cash.

YOU GET TO KEEP MORE OF THE WEALTH YOU CREATE

The benefit of proof is that you keep more of the wealth created by avoiding or delaying VC. Table 8 shows the percentage of wealth retained by 22 billion-dollar entrepreneurs in relation to the wealth created by the ventures they developed.

TABLE 8. WEALTH RETAINED/WEALTH CREATED PERCENTAGE FOR BILLION-DOLLAR ENTREPRENEURS

	VC-FAVORED	VC-DELAYER	VC-AVOIDER
Wealth retained/ wealth created	7%	16%	52%

This table shows the net worth of the entrepreneur as a proportion of the market value of the venture they developed. Even though many entrepreneurs have diversified their portfolio, the assumption is that their net worth is a function of their percent of ownership in the venture. The data is for 22 billion-dollar entrepreneurs whose net worth and venture valuation was available from public sources (in 2011). Although this is for only 22 of the 85 billion-dollar entrepreneurs, it is likely that the percent for VC-avoiders is higher since the percent of wealth retained is likely to be higher for those who stay private and own it themselves, as many do.

Entrepreneurs who want to retain more of the wealth they create should reduce VC involvement. Postponing or avoiding VC increases the proportion of wealth kept. Table 8 shows that the "wealth retained/wealth created" ratio is higher when the VC risk, and level of VC involvement, is lower. VC-avoiders kept 52 percent of the wealth they created compared with 7 percent for those who got VC early, while VC-delayers were in the middle with 16 percent. By building momentum before seeking VC, billion-dollar entrepreneurs reduced dilution to VCs and avoided sharing wealth with VC-recruited CEOs. Entrepreneurs who want to keep more of the wealth they create should avoid VC if they can, or delay it until their business momentum attracts VCs, allowing them to negotiate a more favorable agreement and stay on as the leader.

YOU MAY NEED LESS CAPITAL TO GROW

VCs have a time deadline. They must show that they can earn high *annual* returns on the money entrusted to them, which usually translates to earning a high multiple on their investment in a short time. To succeed, VCs invest heavily to support a full-fledged management team, add significant levels of overhead for anticipated sales, and accept losses by spending heavily on marketing to push customers to buy. Entrepreneurs who wish to avoid or delay venture capital will need to keep their expenses under control and grow their overhead as the business grows, thus keeping cash flow positive.

This means that capital-smart entrepreneurs have no money to lose and to risk. By going slow until the model is proven (see Figure 10), entrepreneurs can make each dollar productive and not risk huge sums of cash—cash that is difficult to raise. By going slow until Aha, billion-dollar entrepreneurs avoided a negative cash flow. When they reached the stage where their potential was evident and they could find financing at a lower cost without losing control, they obtained that additional financing and started to grow.

Mark Zuckerberg grew with family financing and angel financing until his potential was so evident to VCs that he got funding from venture capital funds who allowed him to vote their shares.

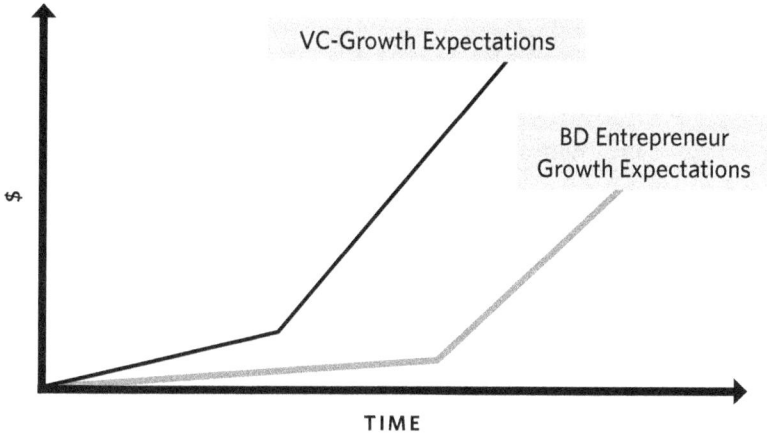

Figure 10. Growth expectations of VCs and billion-dollar entrepreneurs

This means that you need to bridge the credibility gap and the capital gap between idea and Aha! The higher the risk, the higher the target return demanded by investors. Professional venture investors seek target annual returns of 80 to 100 percent for ventures at the research and development stage. By advancing the stage of the venture, entrepreneurs reduce risk and can get investors to settle for lower annual returns due to the increased attractiveness of the venture and attract more investors. The best way to reduce risk for investors is to advance to the next stage with little cash. The stages and risks are as follows:

- At the research and development stage, all risks exist, including whether the product will be developed as planned and on budget. More importantly, investors will wonder whether the product will add value for customers and a competitive advantage when it is ready for commercialization.

- At the startup stage, product risks are reduced. But other risks exist, including whether or not anyone will buy and the margins attained, if the strategy is right for the business, and if the management is right.

- At the emerging stage, investors worry about if sales will grow and if the venture will take off.

- At the growth stage, the questions are whether the growth rate and profitability will continue or not, whether the company will dominate its industry or not, and if there is an attractive exit strategy for investors.

At each stage, more investors may be willing to invest, and at higher valuations, if there is proof of success in the next stage. For example, getting confirmed orders from customers may be a good strategy at startup. Some key suggestions to improve credibility include the following:

- Get independent, credible, and favorable market research to show that you will achieve your sales goals and that a market exists. Asking your friends what they think of your proposed business might not always get a candid response or offer a realistic direction, because they may sugarcoat the truth, often because they may not want to kill your dream or be rude.

- Try "real research" for credibility. This means try to get real orders, accompanied by cash or contractual commitments. This is easier in a business that sells to other businesses. If strong business customers are willing to give conditional contracts, you may have some form of advantage. It is more difficult to do real research in businesses that sell to consumers, but even here, test marketing with smaller numbers may be better than betting the farm on instinct.

- Sometimes it is difficult to predict the size of the markets, especially for revolutionary products and services. Most customers may not switch to a revolutionary product until it has been tested and proved. A survey of potential customers about the likelihood of buying your product or service may only offer guesses, especially if your offering is revolutionary. In such cases, it may be prudent to try different business models with small investments in each, or to spread the risk with an alliance.

Sam Walton tested various business models for 12 years before settling on the one that made Walmart an iconic company.

YOU WILL NOT WASTE AN OPPORTUNITY, BUT ON THE OTHER HAND . . .

You have some choices. You can gamble on your opportunity and "bet the farm," or you could seek a safer road by growing in small steps. But someone may bet everything based on instincts and win the lottery. In general, however, it may be prudent to test your strategies and other key decisions before gambling. This way you will not waste an opportunity.

YOU CAN REDUCE YOUR HIGH-RISK INVESTMENT

Until the Internet era, most VCs invested in companies that sold to other businesses, due to the cost of selling to large national or global consumer markets. Also, the investment needed to reach national consumer markets, including discounts and stocking fees for distribution and retail channels, is often daunting and involves a higher risk than is acceptable to many venture capitalists. So know the cost of proving and operating your business model.

Mark Knudson of Venturi Group is an entrepreneur in the medical industry. Developing new medical products often requires hundreds of millions in capital, so Knudson is usually forced to seek VC. But he reduces risk by developing the "critical experiment" and proving that the product will work in real-life conditions—while he still has money in the bank.

• • •

Finding the right business strategy is one of the most important aspects of growing without capital. History shows that you are not likely to find the right model on the first try. Keep testing various alternatives based on new trends, new needs, new markets, and new competitors and their strategies.

PART IV

THE COMPLETE ENTREPRENEUR: PERSONAL DEVELOPMENT TO GROW MORE WITH LESS

CHAPTER 21

Becoming the Complete Entrepreneur

Glen Taylor started as an intern at a small printing company and today owns one of the largest printing companies in the country. His growth shows how finance-smart entrepreneurs can build a giant and create a fortune with control and without venture capital.

"Why should I succeed when others don't?"
—Glen Taylor, Taylor Corporation

The best way to close this book is to end with the inspiring tale of Glen Taylor, who is one of the most complete entrepreneurs I interviewed.[1] His story is inspirational and educational.

Getting Started on the Right Path

When Glen Taylor was sixteen, he was a father, husband, manager of a farm, and had a 4.0 GPA as a high-school student (if you don't count typing). When he finished high school, his teachers persuaded him to enter college rather than go into farming. With scholarships, loans, and a part-time (32 hours a week) job in a printing company, Taylor pursued a degree in math, which he completed in three years. At the printing company, he implemented so many profitable, commonsense improvements that, upon graduation, the owner asked him to join the company as his number-two guy for an annual salary of under $5,000. Taylor listened to his advisors at his college and joined the printing company, even though he would have made more as a teacher and would have had his summers off. His professors told him that challenging opportunities in business do not show up every day, and he could always go into teaching later.

Within a few years, he had made so many improvements to the company (and asked for a piece of the pie) that he was making in excess of $35,000 and had bought 13 percent of the company with his savings (he could still live on the original $5,000 salary). That is when the owner of the printing company announced that he was ready to sell, giving Taylor a year to put together an offer.

Initially, Taylor planned to buy the company with two of his colleagues. However, he soon found that they had differing goals. Taylor wanted to expand, and expand, and expand. The others did not. So Taylor bought the company on his own. Today his company is a colossus in the printing industry with operations throughout the world, putting Taylor on the Forbes 400 list of richest Americans. He also owns the controlling interest in the Minnesota Timberwolves NBA basketball team.

When Taylor bought the company at the age of 33, he asked himself a basic question: *"Why should we succeed when so many others fail?"* His question is noteworthy due to its timing—when he had already attained what many would think would be a lifetime's worth of success and achievement. The answer helped him land a spot on the Forbes 400.

These are Taylor's six rules on how to grow by controlling capital.

#1: CUSTOMERS MATTER MORE THAN ASSETS

Customer happiness (not just satisfaction) should be foremost on every entrepreneur's mind. If you look at business today, many companies pay lip service to this rule. Corporate executives may disregard this rule because their salaries and options depend on their performance over the next few quarters. They can benefit by cutting employees and service for short-term gain. However, this is not true for entrepreneurs. Your net worth and reputation depend on the long-term happiness of your customers. If your best customers leave, the profits from the next few quarters will not make up for the destruction of your business. If you are not seeking customer happiness, your competitors will seek to make them happier and take your business. Happier customers keep coming back. Happier customers tell others. Happier customers pay more. And that should make you happier.

Here are four marketing strategies that helped Taylor dominate.

Focus on why your customers will buy from you

After joining the wedding-invitation printing industry, Taylor decided to "go against the best and be better than them." So he and his staff laid their competitors' attractive catalogs next to their own and asked the billion-dollar question: "Why will people buy from us?" They could not see how they had any obvious advantage, yet they understood that their customers were all local and sought lower prices. So they copied the competitors' fancy, rich-looking catalogs and included products that were commonly featured, assuming that frequent occurrence of a product indicated popularity. They priced the products attractively, decreased production costs, and widened distribution. Sales started growing.

Use pricing to attract customers and increase profits.

Cut prices without a plan and you are likely to fail. Taylor cut prices selectively on comparable products and then cut costs (more on that later). But his company also offered customized products with higher margins. Realizing that higher prices from an unknown company that did not have a perceived competitive advantage would not succeed on comparable items, they set their prices for basic, glitz-free invitations around 5 percent below competitors. But they had higher prices on accompanying items and customized options. The price of the total package was comparable to that of its competitors, but they were thought of as competitively priced. As an example, matching reception cards, thank-you notes, and reception napkins that competitors did not carry were priced for higher profits.

Innovate to make customers happier, and they will pay more

Innovate to satisfy customers' unmet needs, not to sell what you want to push. With the new catalog, customers and retailers started paying more attention to Taylor. Brides were impressed and placed Taylor's company alongside the leading invitation printers. Taylor noted an increasing number of customer requests for custom designs, wording, and colors to reflect their personalities on their special day. Previously, the industry's response had been to tell them that "you can get what we have." However, Taylor noticed that price was not an issue when the brides wanted to satisfy their unique wishes. So the company tried to satisfy these customers. Previously, Taylor was the low-priced vendor. Now, they started selling customized products at a higher price.

Realizing that this could be a unique advantage, they decided to find what really made their customers happy, and they started to focus on answering the broader question, "What does the bride want?" They hired a designer to create new types of invitations. All innovations and new designs were tested with groups of local female college students, employees, and other young women for feedback. They specially organized these groups to make sure that their innovations were in sync with the market. They could not keep up with demand. Their goal was a minimum of 10 percent gross margins. By differentiating their offerings to satisfy the unique needs of their customers, they increased the size of the typical order by 20 percent and increased profits by over 100 percent. The company started to take off.

At this time, Taylor was approached by an entrepreneur for help in starting a business to supply school proms with products based on the hit songs and movies of the day. Taylor offered to supply him with a variety of paper-based items. When this business took off, Taylor borrowed the concept for wedding invitations. The invitation industry had been built on religious themes, such as a Catholic wording or a Protestant wording. But Taylor's market was similar to that of the entrepreneur. Brides were not much older than the high school graduates who attended proms, and they listened to the same songs and watched the same movies. Taylor came up with new wording and themes based on hit songs and movies. Brides liked these themes, and they further customized their invitations with their own words at a slightly higher cost.

Put customers ahead of assets

Customers pay you to serve their own needs, not to make you more efficient. Since machinery is the most expensive investment in a printing business, Taylor knew that his business needed to be efficient and use printing presses optimally, with flexibility and reduced setup costs. So they modified the machinery and adjusted their business practices. While other printers emphasized machinery utilization and asked customers to adjust (by not accepting smaller orders), Taylor adjusted printing operations to profit from unique orders.

#2. ADD COMPETENCE AS THE BUSINESS GROWS

As your business grows, you need to grow with it. Otherwise, someone else will become better and take away your business. Keep in mind that the slowest gazelle gets eaten. If you are not dominant, someone else is, and you will dance to their tune.

To become dominant, focus on three rungs of leadership growth. The first rung is you—the leader. The second rung is your team. The third rung is to build leaders in your organization who can build their own teams and businesses within your organization. The last is the most difficult if you want to build a business giant. That is why billion-dollar entrepreneurs are rare.

Here are four organizational strategies that helped Taylor dominate.

Never stop learning

If you "know it all," someone will show you that you do not. Continuous personal growth is mandatory if you want to dominate. You need to develop startup skills to launch a business and leadership skills to grow the business. As the company grew, Taylor realized that they had to recruit and develop team members, learn strategy development, and understand how new technologies could be used for customer happiness and company productivity. As an example, they became better at computers and at using them in the business, with help from IBM. To learn how to lead and dominate, Taylor encouraged his senior team to attend executive education programs.

Find potential talent when you cannot afford proven talent

Taylor could not afford to hire experienced corporate employees with proven track records. So his company hired new, young, hungry graduates from Minnesota State University in Mankato. They recruited and trained them to become better managers. They then developed their leadership skills and built the great team that would help them to dominate the industry.

To grow, delegate; to dominate, delegate responsibly

As the business grew, they saw more acquisition opportunities. The industry was consolidating, and weaker companies were being acquired. Many of these opportunities were geographically distant, and Taylor could not manage them from headquarters even if he wanted to do so. So he decided to run each company as its own profit center, and he told the managers that they should run each company as if they owned it. Before giving them this authority, however, he developed some rules. He would only hire people from within the company or people they knew. These included college classmates who had joined large companies and had acquired corporate discipline, then were offered an opportunity to grow with Taylor.

Initially, Taylor would delegate in small steps and made sure that his different companies developed a plan together, which he would closely monitor. He always heard, "Don't you trust me?" from every one of his managers because he checked everything in the early stages of the manager's tenure. Taylor's response was, "Yes, I trust you, but I want to check for the first few years because I want you running this business for a lifetime." Taylor believed in "over-managing for the first few years and under-managing later." After developing a degree of comfort with the managers, he would "under-manage" and receive monthly financial statements, a report of whatever they wanted to talk about, and an annual budget. They got the background before the budget so they were aware of the situation before seeing the numbers. Taylor called the managers only if there were surprises.

Six words to build a great team: *You* did well. *We* screwed up.

All major decisions were made after discussing all the details with the manager and others who were affected. Once they made a decision, Taylor would tell them, "We back you and support you. We are in this together." If something went wrong, they took joint responsibility and went straight to finding a solution. Taylor never sought to assign blame and never said, "I told you so" to the managers. This gave the managers the comfort to admit any mistakes quickly and to find a solution before the mistake became a cancer.

#3. SURF WITH THE TRENDS

A wise sage once said, "Executives can be undertakers, caretakers, or risk takers."

The problem is that undertakers bury the dead, caretakers bury the living, and risk takers bury themselves. By not adapting to and exploiting opportunities as the world changes, caretakers think they are minimizing risks even as they fall behind competitors and send their businesses spiraling to their doom. As W. Edwards Deming said, "You don't have to change. Survival is not mandatory." Risk takers bury themselves, because the key to success is not assuming huge risks but exploiting opportunities while minimizing risks.

The venture capitalist Tom Perkins said that the "key to Kleiner Perkins's success was determining a venture's risk, then attempting to eliminate it." Eliminating risks is not easy since, to do so, you have to forecast perfectly. Relying on forecasters can be dangerous. As Edgar R. Fiedler noted, "The herd instinct among forecasters makes sheep look like independent thinkers."

Here are four growth strategies that helped Taylor dominate.

Stay on top of trends

Taylor was always seeking ways to improve connection with customers and to serve their needs more efficiently by finding any small competitive edge they could find. When they noticed that their focus groups and customers wanted unique colors, they asked the mills for customized colors. To supply customized colors, the paper manufacturers wanted large minimum orders. So Taylor had to know which colors would sell. Taylor employees started attending the New York bridal shows to examine the latest fashions and colors. Their customers could now coordinate their wedding colors, including paper products, invitations, bridal dresses, etc. and be "cool." Sales and profits took off.

Expand with your strength

To grow, Taylor expanded its distribution network from its regional base. In addition to expanding geographically, they also added Hallmark card stores, florists, printing shops, and bridal shops. Previously, they could only ship via the U.S. Postal Service, which resulted in a high level of damage. Since UPS was expanding into rural America, and Taylor had always been happy with UPS, they decided to expand their market based on UPS expansion plans. As UPS expanded its geographic reach one state at a time, so did Taylor. Now, Taylor's company offered faster service. Chicago and New York printers normally shipped in fourteen days. While Taylor shipped products on the same day for rush orders (at a slightly higher price, of course), all orders were shipped within two days. No one was faster. With customization and speed, sales shot up and so did profit margins.

Plan for downdrafts

Soon after Taylor's acquisition of Carlson and a second company in Indiana, there was a scare about a potential paper shortage. All printers were expected to get a reduced, but proportionate, share of paper, potentially shrinking the core invitation-printing business. To prevent this, Taylor found an envelope company in trouble and purchased it at a reasonable price. The plan was to shut it down and use its paper quota to protect the core business. But the shortage never materialized, and the scare was unfounded. Taylor had obtained seller financing for the envelope-company purchase with a small down payment and found that they had another profitable business.

Use the proven formula to grow, as long as the trends don't change

As Taylor grew, more opportunities came his way. Now he could add size to a customer-focused, operationally efficient business. The result was a super-competitive juggernaut. He kept buying competitors, placing strong managers from the team at the helm of the new business, making their marketing more customer focused, improving their operations, and repeating the formula that made Taylor successful. This became the virtuous spiral. They managed "by exception," that is. Managers who needed extra help, or were not performing well, or had not built a successful track record got extra attention.

#4. IMPROVE CONTROLS AS SCOPE GROWS

Leading a business without monitoring the numbers is like driving a car without knowing your direction or speed. You will crash. With a growing business comes more complexity and more ways to make mistakes. Taylor tracked all the important numbers of the business, including the accounting, financial, operations, and marketing numbers, to identify potential problems. Track your customers and make them happier.

Here are four financial strategies that helped Taylor dominate.

Learn finance skills and track your numbers to avoid a crash

First, identify the key numbers that are relevant to *your* business. Start with the financial data, especially cash flow. Undoubtedly cash and cash flow are paramount to the survival of the business. But to succeed and dominate, track your customers, competitors, products, trends and their impacts, and the results of your strategy. Monitor productivity of labor, materials, machines, and other assets. Taylor became more efficient to satisfy his customers and to cut costs. In addition to charging more for smaller orders, the company improved every aspect of the business. For example:

- The company was buying raw materials in packages. These were then unpackaged, printed, repackaged, and sold. They streamlined this process and bought in bulk to reduce the cost of raw materials and the labor cost to open the packages.

- They scheduled the printing by color to minimize press setup time and developed labor and machinery standards to measure and improve individual and company productivity and reduce costs.

- They developed stronger controls to know the cost and proportion of raw materials that were wasted, and then they cut the waste.

Track frequently to avoid surprises and make a difference

As soon as Taylor bought the company in 1975, he hired his first full-time accountant. He hired someone he already knew, and the new accountant expressed surprise at the amount of information the company was collecting. They recorded everything to track the company and to know what was "out of whack." They knew their raw material costs, labor costs, labor productivity, raw-material waste (even some of what was not being reported), overhead, equipment usage, etc. The accounting team added to that base knowledge and implemented systems to allow the company to improve control and predict performance as they continued to grow.

Acquire only if the value is higher than the price

They also tracked other companies in the industry and their problems. Taylor knew that they were ahead of their competitors in improvements and results. When these companies started to become available, Taylor started buying them. When they heard from a competitor in Indiana who was in trouble, he immediately took off to see the potential seller and knocked on his door at two a.m. He already knew enough about the company to make an offer. He knew that the company was smaller, and the catalog was not up to Taylor's standards. He knew that the company was not making a profit because it had too many employees, poor productivity, high levels of waste, and poor employee morale. Most important, he knew that they could fix these problems. The seller wanted $1 million for the business (so his wife would be taken care of if he died). Taylor thought that the price for the business was a little high. He knew that they could pay $900,000 for the business with seller financing, but they could also pay an additional $200,000 for the building that could be financed at a lower rate and amortized over a longer term. Both parties got what they wanted, and the deal was done.

Enjoy the potential but control risks

Large customers can mean big orders, huge investments, and giant risks. *That's why elephants dance with other elephants.* As the company grew, they were able to satisfy the needs of corporate customers. Their goal with these large customers was to "do everything for the customer" to make it difficult for them to switch vendors. Services included design, manufacturing, warehousing, marketing, and fulfillment so they could control the entire process. They often took the upfront risk of starting these companies' programs, as long as they could recoup the investment from the customer, or by adding other customers. They offered total confidentiality so that customer information was never shared with anyone else, which enhanced trust. They kept their prices competitive while simultaneously driving efficiencies in operations to increase profitability. And they could offer management stability and continuity, while larger companies had high turnover. This allowed them to minimize the risks of change and discontinuity in the customer's program, realize increased efficiencies from experience, and make long-term commitments.

If the customer demands became unprofitable, however, Taylor was always prepared to walk away. The company hedged risks by having backup strategies for their major investments. On occasion, they found themselves facing a lower bid from a competitor to steal a key account. When this happened, they offered rock-bottom prices to capture the competitor's key customers. The competitor got the message.

#5. SMART FINANCE IS SMARTER THAN SMART MONEY

What is better: easy money or smart finance? Easy money sounds tempting as a "no-lose" proposition—you get lots of money from investors (hopefully with few strings and a great venture valuation), you control and grow your business, earn a high salary, and sell your shares in an "irrationally exuberant" market for billions. The reality is that few ventures live this dream. Home runs like Google and Facebook are extremely rare; they primarily occur in hot, emerging industries and in few geographic areas, such as Silicon Valley. You may have a better chance of winning the lottery.

Smart finance involves knowing and understanding the pros and cons of your financing options and developing a plan that is right for you and your company. In Taylor's opinion, the best financing source for most companies is internal cash flow from operations. It can allow you to keep more of the company and to stay in control.

Here are three financing strategies that helped Taylor dominate.

Increase internal cash flow to get more external finance

The more internal cash flow you have, the more external financing you are likely to get. Internal cash flow is money you control, which is key when dealing with financiers. If financiers control, you can often lose. So find ways to increase internal cash flow by becoming capital-efficient. Taylor's philosophy was, "It's not just how much money you make, it is how much you keep." To increase internal cash flow, Taylor cut waste, reduced the cash-to-cash cycle, made sure that each dollar earned its targeted return, helped employees improve productivity, and kept margins high.

Find the right external financing and financing structure

You can "fill the gaps" with the right types, sources, and levels of external financing. Find sources that balance cost with flexibility. Government sources can be the cheapest, followed by bank loans (if you don't count the cost of the personal guarantee they demand). Getting equity can be expensive from a financial perspective and also from a control perspective. Taylor always sought the cheapest financing he could get. When they expanded, Taylor sought financing from local and state government sources because they often were the cheapest, and the subordinated nature of many government loans also encouraged private financial institutions to offer funds at a lower cost. While Taylor sought extended terms from his financiers, his company also improved operations and paid the debt back quickly. They never borrowed more than they could repay, even under their most pessimistic scenario.

Use seller financing for acquisitions

In acquisitions, which Taylor did frequently, he knew that the best financing was from the sellers. When Taylor bought Carlson Craft, he first arranged financing from the bank and then sought seller financing because he preferred this option rather than money from the bank (as noted earlier, Taylor and two of his assistants were offered the deal by the seller—but the other two did not want growth—so Taylor offered to buy their shares also and made a deal with them). He offered rates that were higher than bank rates for deposits and lower than bank rates on loans. Taylor structured the loan with a longer term, with the option of extending it if needed. He always paid off the loan before it was due. All parties benefited. He followed a similar strategy and accomplished the same result when he made his first external acquisition. The strategy worked well for both parties. Sellers were flexible in the financing they offered, which fit Taylor's business strategy.

#6. *I* DIDN'T DO THIS. *WE* DID

It is difficult to recruit proven talent when you are a young, untested company with few resources. Joining is risky for talented people who usually have other options. But without great people on your team, your business can only grow to the limit of your own talents. So identify the right people and recruit them by enabling them to reach their own potential as you reach your goals.

Here are four leadership strategies to build a dominating team.

Practice the golden rule

As the old saying goes, "Bulls make money, bears make money, but hogs don't." To make your team work harder for you than your competitors' employees work for them, find the congruence of interests—where your interests and that of your team are aligned—so that they will do their best even when you are not looking over their shoulder. When Taylor first heard of "win-win," he wondered, "What kind of pinkie idea is this?" But he realized that when he worked to benefit managers, employees, customers, and vendors as teams, all did well when compared with deals where one did well and the others did not. They realized that they could be more successful by getting a smaller share of a larger pie than by hogging a larger share of a smaller pie. People work for their self-interest. The key is to blend yours with theirs. Make them rich if they are making you rich.

Customize the rewards

Each manager marches to a different drummer. To have a greater impact, customize the incentive plan for each person on your team according to their unique personality and position. Taylor found that incentives produced results, so he made sure that there were systems to motivate and also to prevent abuse. Taylor's incentive system offered a significant share of any increase in profits in the first year, but the company kept a large share of the profits from subsequent years at that level. Managers got a percentage of their salary as bonuses, and this percentage went as high as 200 percent of their salary. The normal range was between 50 and 75 percent. The managers received 100 percent of the goal if they met their budget, and they could get up to 200 percent if they found a unique way to make money. This offered a huge incentive to do better. The next year they got a base bonus based on the higher platform. Each company's bonus was based on its own reality. If company A was in a bad economy, the base was reduced. If company B could get a competitor's business, the managers were paid a higher bonus. Taylor found that some do try to "sandbag" (seek lower performance targets because they claim that "business conditions are worse this year" and then try to get bonuses based on this lowered base), and the same people seem to try it year after year. Taylor believed in knowing the people with whom he worked. If he knew someone was sandbagging, he raised the stakes—they needed to reach a higher proportion of the budget before they qualified for bonuses. In addition, if at the end of the year, the managers did "non-normal" things to meet their thresholds for bonuses, he reserved the right to adjust. As an example, if they cut advertising budgets to get bonuses, then their threshold was adjusted because the following year's performance could suffer. Taylor also found that some employees (the "dreamers") set goals higher than they should. He let them set dream goals since he did not want to demotivate them. But in these cases, he set the bonus at under 100 percent of budget.

Be loyal if you expect loyalty

When Taylor bought the envelope company (mentioned earlier), he had to find the right manager for the company. One of his key employees had an autistic baby, and he knew that the baby could have access to more health-care resources in the larger Twin Cities metro area, where the envelope company was located, than in Mankato, where Taylor has its headquarters. He offered the employee the opportunity to move to the Twin Cities to manage this company so the family could find more resources and greater opportunities for their child. This employee was not the most experienced manager among Taylor's options, but he eventually turned out to be one of the best in the company.

Tie rewards to productivity

To increase productivity, Taylor first developed standards for employees and machines and then found ways to up the productivity. The company analyzed operations and then simplified them to gain efficiencies. They monitored their divisions and their key components every day. This included orders, shipments, and production. They instituted information systems even before the prevalence of computers by developing a card system to keep track of the key data they needed. All supervisors had to know the productivity for each of the people they managed at the end of each day.

There were four pay scales (A,B,C,D) based on production. Employees started at the lowest scale and were promoted to higher pay scales as their productivity improved. In essence, they were basing pay scales on productivity, rather than on time served. If employees could not maintain their productivity, the supervisor would assist them. If they needed a slower pace, they were moved to another job at a lower pay scale. Production employees were also offered a profit-sharing system tied to their individual companies (not to the parent Taylor Corporation), along with a pension fund and a 401(k).

CHAPTER 22

Conclusion

This book defines the billion-dollar entrepreneur (BDE) Way, with smart entrepreneurs, such as Glen Taylor, as the basis for this expertise-driven model of venture growth. It is a "bottom-up" method, which means that the entrepreneur is not waiting to be selected for funding by a VC. This approach is also a model for entrepreneurs who are focused on becoming grade A leaders while developing grade A businesses. By avoiding VC or delaying it, the BDE Way allows entrepreneurs to take off without VC and control the venture and the wealth they have created.

Success is due to entrepreneurial skills and strategies, and entrepreneurs prove their brilliance with their performance—not by writing great plans for VCs.

This book seeks to shatter the belief that entrepreneurs need to follow the VC Way, which is the VC-based, opportunity-driven model built on the premise that entrepreneurs need early-stage venture capital (VC) to build giant businesses. The VC Way is a "top-down" method and is based on finding grade A opportunities and then recruiting grade A executives. Financiers control the venture. Many entrepreneurs assume that they need to use the VC Way to grow, which promotes business plan competitions and Shark-Tank events. But the odds are slim.

This book shows that most entrepreneurs succeed because of their expertise, not because of the idea. Most ideas can be imitated and improved, as was proved by Jobs, Gates, and Zuckerberg. Entrepreneurs need to know how to execute with the right skills and competitive strategies if they want to grow with control of their venture and the wealth created.

Notes

INTRODUCTION

1. Michael Ewens and Matt Marx, "Research: What Happens to a Startup when Venture Capitalists Replace the Founder," *Harvard Business Review*, February 14, 2018

2. Peter Burrows, "He Thinks Different," *Businessweek*, November 1, 2004, p. 20

3. Brad Stone, "Friends with Benefits," *Bloomberg Businessweek*, February 6, 2012

CHAPTER 1

1. Monte Burke, "Kevin Plank's Billionaire Horseowner," *ForbesLife*, September 2012, p. 46

2. Gerard J. Tellis and Peter N. Golder, "Pioneer Advantage: Marketing Logic or Marketing Legend," *Journal of Marketing Research*, 30, no. 2, (May 1993), p. 158

3. Brad Stone, "The Secrets of Bezos," *Bloomberg Businessweek*, October 10, 2013, p. 58

CHAPTER 2

1. Adam Lashinsky, "Jeff Bezos: The Ultimate Disrupter," *Fortune*, December 3, 2012, p. 100

CHAPTER 3

1. Vivienne Walt, "Meet the Third-Richest Man in the World," *Fortune*, January 14, 2013, p. 74

CHAPTER 4

1. Matt Rosoff, "Jeff Bezos Told Me what May Be the Best Startup Investment Ever," BusinessInsider.com, October 20, 2016, http://www.businessinsider.com/jeff-bezos-on-early -amazon-investors-2016-10

2. Max Chafkin, "What Makes Uber Run," FastCompany.com, October 2015, p. 112

3. Microsoft web site, https://news.microsoft.com/2000/05/09/ microsoft-fast-facts-1975/, May 9, 2000

4. Lauren Thomas, "Walmart Is Reportedly Telling Its Tech Vendors to Leave Amazon's Cloud," CNBC.com, June 21, 2017, http:// www.cnbc.com/2017/06/21/wal-mart-is-reportedly-telling-its- tech-vendors-to-leave-amazons-cloud.html

5. Avery Hartmans and Nathan McAlone, "The Story of how Travis Kalanick Built Uber into the Most Feared and Valuable Startup in the World," BusinessInsider.com, August 1, 2016, http://www .businessinsider.com/ubers-history/#december-2008-kalanick -first-hears-the-idea-for-uber-at-the-leweb-technology -conference-he-thinks-of-it-as-a-way-to-lower-the-cost-of -a-black-car-service-using-your-phone-4

6. Brad Stone and Douglas MacMillan, "How Zuckerberg Hacked the Valley," *Bloomberg Businessweek*, March 21, 2012, p. 62

7. Bloomberg L.P., http://en.wikipedia.org/wiki/Bloomberg_L.P.

8. Dileep Rao, "Fastenal: Robert Kierlin," *Bootstrap to Billions*, 2009, www.uentrepreneurs.com

PART 2

1. Peter J. Golder and Gerard J. Tellis, "Pioneer Advantage: Marketing Logic or Marketing Legend," *Journal of Marketing Research*, (May 1993), p. 158

2. Sophie Curtis, "Bill Gates: A History at Microsoft," *The Telegraph*, February 4, 2014, https://www.telegraph.co.uk/technology/bill-gates/10616991/Bill-Gates-a-history-at-Microsoft.html

3. Eli Broad, *The Art of Being Unreasonable: Lessons in Unconventional Thinking*, May 2012, Wiley

4. Douglas Martin, "Rosalia Mera, 69, Cofounder of Zara," The *New York Times Obituaries*, August 22, 2013

CHAPTER 5

1. Data from PwC MoneyTree

2. http://www.pwcmoneytree.com/CurrentQuarter/BySoD

3. David Rubenstein and David Marquardt, https://www.quora.com/How-much-venture-capital-did-Microsoft-raise

4. Bob Zider, "How Venture Capital Works," *Harvard Business Review*, (Nov–Dec 1998), Harvard University

CHAPTER 6

1. Dileep Rao, "Lloyd's Barbeque: Lloyd Sigel, 2009," *Bootstrap to Billions*, www.uentrepreneurs.com

2. Wikipedia, McCaw Cellular, https://en.wikipedia.org/wiki/AT%26T_Wireless_Services#McCaw_Cellular

3. Craig McCaw, https://en.wikipedia.org/wiki/Craig_McCaw, Wikipedia.org

4. Lacey Rose, Shill Shocked, *Forbes*, November 22, 2010, p. 146 and at https://www.forbes.com/forbes/2010/1122/private-companies -10-guthy-renker-media-shill-shocked .html#41e49f37170a

5. Dileep Rao from an interview with Gustavo Cisneros at Florida International University College of Business, 2012

6. Intel Corporation, Encyclopedia.com, https://www.encyclopedia .com/social-sciences-and-law/economics-business-and-labor/businesses-and-occupations/intel-corp

7. Cliff Edwards, "Supercharging Silicon Valley," *Businessweek*, October 4, 2004, p. 18

8. Dileep Rao, "Capella Education Company: Steve Shank," *Bootstrap to Billions*, 2009, www.uentrepreneurs.com

9. Diane Brady, "Gustavo A. Cisneros," *Bloomberg Businessweek*, June 27, 2011

10. Anne VanderMey, "Whole Foods' Quality Crop," *Fortune*, December 3, 2012, p. 24

11. Devon Pendleton, "The Billionaire Behind Chobani," *StarTribune*, September 26, 2012, p. D3

CHAPTER 7

1. Carl Hoffman, "Shooting for the Stars," *Wall Street Journal* Magazine, October 27, 2011, p. 94

2. Dinah Eng, "Adventures of a Serial Entrepreneur," *Fortune*, April 30, 2012, p. 23

3. Dinah Eng, "How Panda Express Brings Chinese Food to the Mall," *Fortune*, February 4, 2013, p. 27

4. Roben Farzad, "Fastenal's Runaway Stock Success," *Bloomberg Businessweek*, February 27, 2012, p. 47

5. Matthew Boyle, "Why Fedex Is Flying High," *Fortune*, November 15, 2004, p. 196

CHAPTER 8

1. Neil Genzlinger, "They Made America: 1 Percent Inspiration, 99 Percent Marketing," *The New York Times*, January 23, 2005 (Sunday Book Review)

2. Dinah Eng, "Secrets of Pilot Flying J's the Truck-Stop King," *Fortune*, October 22, 2012, http://fortune.com/2012/10/22/secrets-of-pilot-flying-js-the-truck-stop-king/

3. Schumpeter, "Pretty Profitable Parrots," *The Economist*, May 12, 2012, http://www.economist.com/node/21554500

4. Interview with Gustavo Cisneros at Florida International University College of Business, 2012

5. Dileep Rao, "Medtronic: Earl Bakken," *Bootstrap to Billions*, Dileep Rao, 2009, www.uentrepreneurs.com

6. Rob Brunner, "America Shacks Up," FastCompany.com, July-August 2015

CHAPTER 9

1. Todd Wenning, "Mark Twain's $4 Million Mistake," *The Motley Fool*, September 16, 2006, http://www.fool.com/investing/high-growth/2006/09/16/mark-twains-4-million-mistake.aspx

CHAPTER 10

1. Elaine Wong, "The Most Memorable Product Launches of 2010," *Forbes* (online), December 3, 2010, http://www.forbes.com/2010/12/03/most-memorable-products-leadership-cmo-network.html

2. Kevin Plank, "How I Did It: Under Armour's Founder on Learning to Leverage Celebrity Endorsements," *Harvard Business Review*, May 2012

3. Dean Foust, "No Overnight Success," *Business Week*, September 20, 2004, p. 18

4. Matthew Herper, "Money, Math and Medicine," *Forbes*, November 22, 2010

5. Dileep Rao, "CNS/Breathe Right: Dan Cohen," *Bootstrap to Billions*, 2009, www.uentrepreneurs.com

6. Duff McDonald, "The Mastermind of Adrenaline Marketing," *Bloomberg Businessweek*, May 23, 2011, p. 66

7. Anne VanderMey, "Whole Foods' Quality Crop," *Fortune*, December 3, 2012, p. 24

8. Monte Burke, "All in the Family," *Forbes*, August 6, 2012, p. 93

9. Andy Serwer, "Steve Jobs vs. Sam Walton: The Tale of the Tape," *Fortune*, December 3, 2012, p. 123

10. Adam Lashinsky, "Amazon's Jeff Bezos: The Ultimate Disruptor," *Fortune*, December 3, 2012, p. 104

11. Quentin Hardy, "Power in the Numbers," *Forbes*, May 24, 2010, p. 18

CHAPTER 11

1. Steven C. Wheelwright and Edward Smith, The New Product Development Imperative, *Harvard Business Review*, March 4, 1999, HBS 9-699-152

2. Beth Kowitt, "A Founder's Bold Gamble on Panera," *Fortune*, August 13, 2012, p. 19

3. Stefan Thomke and Barbara Feinberg, "Design Thinking and Innovation at Apple," Harvard Business School case, January 2009 (Revised March 2012), 609–066

CHAPTER 12

1. Gary Rivlin, "Segway's Breakdown," *Wired*, March 1, 2003, http://www.wired.com/wired/archive/11.03/segway_pr.html

2. George Anders, "You're Never Too Old to Get Rich Again," *Forbes*, October 7, 2013, p. 80

3. Ashlee Vance, "The Two Horsemen of the Enterprise Software Apocalypse," *Bloomberg Businessweek*, June 18, 2012, p. 54

4. Dileep Rao, "Aveda: Horst Rechelbacher," *Bootstrap to Billions*, Dileep Rao, 2009, www.uentrepreneurs.com

5. Christopher Tkaczyk, "The Best Ideas Come from the Front Line," *Fortune*, November 15, 2004, p. 196

6. Dileep Rao, "Aveda: Horst Rechelbacher," *Bootstrap to Billions*, Dileep Rao, 2009, www.uentrepreneurs.com

7. Dileep Rao, "Fastenal: Robert Kierlin", *Bootstrap to Billions*, Dileep Rao, 2009, www.uentrepreneurs.com

PART 3

1. Bill Gates, "How Much Venture Capital Did Microsoft Raise," Quora, November 15, 2015, https://www.quora.com/How-much-venture-capital-did-Microsoft-raise

2. Dileep Rao, *Avoid VC Intelligently*, 2015, p. 16. www.uentrepreneurs.com

CHAPTER 13

1. Dileep Rao, *Avoid VC Intelligently*, 2015, p. 55, www.uentrepreneurs.com

2. Dileep Rao, *Bootstrap to Billions*, 2009, www.uentrepreneurs.com

CHAPTER 15

1. W. Chan Kim and Renee Mauborgne, "Value Innovation: The Strategic Logic of High Growth," *Harvard Business Review*, July 2004

2. Dileep Rao, "Tastefully Simple: Jill Blashack Strahan," *Bootstrap to Billions*, 2009, p. 227, www.uentrepreneurs.com

3. Dileep Rao, "Venturi Group: Mark Knudson, *Bootstrap to Billions*, 2009, p. 281, www.uentrepreneurs.com

4. Sridhar Pappu, "What's Next for Michael Bloomberg," FastCompany.com, September, 2011, p. 128

5. Dileep Rao, "Northern Tool & Equipment: Don Kotula," *Bootstrap to Billions*, 2009, p. 178, www.uentrepreneurs.com

6. Dileep Rao, "Aveda: Horst Rechelbacher," *Bootstrap to Billions*, 2009, p. 1, www.uentrepreneurs.com

CHAPTER 16

1. Sam Walton and John Huey, *Sam Walton: Made in America*, 1992, Doubleday

2. Dileep Rao, "Navarre: Eric Paulson," *Bootstrap to Billions*, 2009, www.uentrepreneurs.com

3. Don Martin and Renee Martin, *The Risk Takers: 16 Women and Men Share their Entrepreneurial Strategies for Success*, 2010, Vanguard Press

CHAPTER 17

1. Dileep Rao, "Viromed/Apptec: Bonnie Baskin," *Bootstrap to Billions*, 2009, www.uentrepreneurs.com

CHAPTER 18

1. Rob Brunner, "How Chobani's Hamdi Ulukaya is Winning America's Culture War, *Fast Company*, March 20, 2017, p. 38

2. "Tony Hsieh: Redefining Zappos' Business Model," *Business week*, May 31, 2010, p. 88, https://www.bloomberg.com/news/articles/2010-05-27/tony-hsieh-redefining-zappos-business-model

3. Dileep Rao, "CSM Corporation: Gary Holmes," *Bootstrap to Billions*, 2009, www.uentrepreneurs.com

CHAPTER 19

1. Pablo Bachelet, *Gustavo Cisneros, Pioneer*, p. 165, Hispanic Publishing LLC, 2004

2. Jordan Crook, "Netflix Learns from Past Mistakes, Increases Prices the Right Way," TechCrunch, May 9, 2014, http://techcrunch.com

/2014/05/09/netflix-learns-from-past-mistakes-increases-prices
-the-right-way/

3. David W. Fuller, Tim Talevich and Brenda Shecter, "The Empire Built on Values," *The Costco Connection*, January 2012, p. 24

4. Stephan Faris, "Ground Zero: A Starbucks-free Italy," *Bloomberg Businessweek*, February 9, 2012, https://www.bloomberg.com/news/articles/2012-02-09/grounds-zero-a-starbucks-free-italy

5. Dileep Rao, "Modern Merchandising: Harold Roitenberg," *Bootstrap to Billions*, 2009, www.uentrepreneurs.com

CHAPTER 20

1. Janet Guyon, "The Magic Touch," *Fortune*, September, 6, 2004, p. 236

2. Paul Chaney, "Are Startup Failure Rates as Bad as They Used to Be? *Small Business Trends*, August 7, 2016, https://smallbiztrends.com/2016/08/are-startup-failure-rates-still-bad.html

3. Mary Vinnedge, "Richard Branson: Virgin Entrepreneur," *Success* magazine, May 31, 2009, https://www.success.com/article/richard-branson-virgin-entrepreneur

4. Dileep Rao, "Capella Education Company: Steve Shank," *Bootstrap to Billions*, 2009, www.uentrepreneurs.com

5. Max Chafkin, "Not Just Another Web 2.0 Company, Yelp Basks in its Start Power," *Fast Company*, December 2012/January 2013, p. 91

6. Karl Ulrich's talk at the University of Minnesota, "Developing New-Category Products," Allen D. Shocker Lecture, March 3, 2004, http://www.npdbd.umn.edu/useful-links/shocker-lecture/shocker-lecture-2004

7. Randy Alfred, "April 4, 1975: Bill Gates, Paul Allen Form a

Little Partnership," *Wired*, April 4, 2008, https://www.wired.com/2008/04/dayintech-0404/

CHAPTER 21

1. Dileep Rao, "Taylor Corporation: Glen Taylor," *Bootstrap to Billions*, 2009, www.uentrepreneurs.com

About the Author

Dileep Rao, PhD, was vice president of financing and business development and a board member at a venture development and finance institution for twenty-three years, where he financed the growth of hundreds of businesses and real estate projects.

Dr. Rao has started four businesses (including corporate ventures) and managed five turnaround businesses (four succeeded) where he was chairman and director of emerging ventures and financial institutions.

Dr. Rao advises on building big businesses with finance-smart strategies. His clients have included entrepreneurs; governments, including the US government; Fortune 1000 corporations, including Medtronic and General Mills; and financial institutions, such as banks and development finance institutions in the United States.

Dr. Rao is a clinical professor of entrepreneurship at Florida International University. He has also taught at INCAE (Costa Rica), Stanford University, in the MBA and Executive MBA programs at the University of Minnesota (UM), Carlson School of Management, where he was a three-time Outstanding MBA Teacher of the Year, and in executive MBA programs in Europe, Latin America, and Asia.

He also is a keynote speaker on how finance-smart entrepreneurs and executives develop high-growth ventures without venture capital.

Dr. Rao is a nationally acclaimed author and the entrepreneurship and entrepreneurial finance blogger for Forbes.com, one of the world's largest online business sites. He has two engineering degrees and a doctorate in business administration from the University of Minnesota.